WHY DO MEN HAVE NIPPLES?

WHY DO MEN HAVE NIPPLES?

AND OTHER LOW-LIFE ANSWERS TO REAL-LIFE QUESTIONS

KATHERINE DUNN

Formerly published as *THE SLICE*

WARNER BOOKS

A Time Warner Company

Warner Books Edition
Copyright © 1990 by Katherine Dunn
All rights reserved.
This Warner Books edition is published by arrangement with the author.

Warner Books, Inc., 1271 Avenue of the Americas, New York, NY 10020

 A Time Warner Company

Printed in the United States of America
First Warner Books Printing: November 1992
10 9 8 7 6 5 4 3 2 1

Library of Congress Cataloging in Publication Data

Dunn, Katherine.
[Slice]
Why do men have nipples? : and other low-life answers to real-life questions / Katherine Dunn. —Warner Books ed.
p.   cm.
A collection of questions taken from the author's column in the Willamette week.
Originally published: The slice. Portland, Or. : W W Press, c1990.
ISBN 0-446-39412-2
1. American wit and humor.   2. Questions and answers.   I. Title.
PN6163.D86   1992
814'.54—dc20
92-13888
CIP

Cover design by Diane Luger
Cover illustration by Sandra Fillipucci

CONTENTS

INTRODUCTION:
Information with an Attitude

THE MOST FREQUENTLY ASKED QUESTIONS ABOUT THE SLICE

Q: What is The Slice? How did it come to be? Why is it called The Slice?

A: The Slice is an opinionated question-and-answer column that appears in *Willamette Week*, the alternative weekly newspaper in Portland, Oregon. The topics range from local puzzles such as how long your jail sentence would be for shooting the birds on the Broadway Bridge to cosmic mysteries such as why men have nipples and how the toilet on the space shuttle actually works.

The Slicer, born with a pathological curiosity about almost everything, delights in this excuse to indulge her info-mania. Two subjects have always been off limits: cooking and domestic relations. The Slicer's disinterest and ineptitude in both sports suggests that questions on these topics should be directed to more capable hands.

The column exists because *W.W.* editor Mark Zusman wanted some way for the readers to communicate with and participate in his newspaper. The original reason The Slicer accepted the assignment was a hole in her bank acount. The reason she goes on doing it is that intriguing mail and a tax-deductible excuse to go anywhere and ask anybody anything is addictive.

The column is called The Slice because that word can mean many things, from slice as in wound or as in golf to slice of pie or slice of life. The Slicer invented this title in desperation because the editor wanted to call the column "The Straight Poop." This writer did not relish the idea of bushels of mail addressed to "The Pooper."

Q: Who really writes the questions?
A: Before beginning work on this column, The Slicer suspected that Dear Abby, Ann Landers and Miss Manners all wrote their own questions. The letters seemed too weird, witty and well written to have come in from the real world. Now The Slicer knows better. The questions actually do arrive on cards and in letters from readers. That means fifty percent of the work is already done. It would be silly to overlook that advantage.

Q: Isn't it pretentious to refer to yourself in the third person?
A: Yes, indeed. And unlike Oliver North, various politicians and several professional athletes, The Slicer thinks it's funny.

Q: Why didn't you answer my question?
A: Maybe you stumped The Slicer. Though every letter is read and considered, space in the column is limited and The Slicer is a mere ragtag mortal. Decisions on which questions to answer are based on what seems important to a lot of readers, what tweaks The Slicer's personal curiosity and whether she can find an answer. Sometimes a letter will sit in the files for a year before The Slicer stumbles on the clue that leads to a solution.

There are also letters—and these often contain fascinating questions—which, despite the wide latitude allowed by the First

Amendment, are unprintable. Their libelous remarks or unsubstantiated allegations of criminality could send The Slicer directly to the receiving end of a lawsuit. No, thanks. But when appropriate these items are passed on to investigative reporters in the *W.W.* newsroom for further study.

Q: Has The Slicer made any big discoveries?
A: Certainly. Thousands. But the greatest revelation for The Slicer is that no subject is boring if you are willing to look below the surface. Even bookkeeping, outrageous though this may sound, can be fascinating if you talk to the right impassioned expert.

This volume is a collection of some of the questions that have most intrigued, plagued or entertained The Slicer. May they do the same for you.

1 Get Physical

BOOTHILL HAIRSTYLES

Q: My grandmother is a zesty woman of 80, and I adore her, but she keeps telling me that hair and nails on a human corpse continue to grow after death. She claims to have seen the results herself in the bodies of her husband and her son (my dad). She says, "They had three-inch claws like a Chinee lord when we sank 'em in the hill." Gran also swears that both men died with crew cuts but were buried with Elvis-style long hair that the morticians greased into DAs ["duck's ass"—a hoodlum-style hairdo from the '50s]. Never having seen a dead person, I still find myself wondering if this can possibly be true. I don't intend to fight with Gran about it one way or another, but I'd like to know.

— *Granny's Boy*

A: Not to impugn the veracity of anybody's Granny, but this is raw hooey. Dr. Larry Lewman, Oregon's state medical examiner, says it's not true, but it may, to a small extent, appear to be true. What sometimes happens is that the skin surrounding the hairs or nails dries out and retracts after death. The hair doesn't actually grow, but a little more is visible at the root. Lewman says we're talking about about a quarter of an inch here. Not three inches.

W.W.'s resident archaeologist, Angie Jabine, hypothesizes that the myth of post-mortem hair growth might have been spawned by the growth, under some circumstances, of moss on bones.

MENS' NIPPLES

Q: Why do men have nipples?

— Women Who Want To Know

A: It might be useful, for the sake of illustration, to consider the human body as a standard design, like a Chevy off the assembly line. It has one of two kinds of transmission— automatic or manual—and other details, from paint job to length of eyelash, can be elaborated with optional accessories. This analogy stems from the fact that each human fetus has all the plumbing necessary for either sex; whether it turns out to be a boy or a girl model depends on which hormones kick in. Estrogen produces females; testosterone produces males. The choice of hormones is made when either the X or Y chromosome is contributed by the male sperm fertilizing the ovum. The "Milk Line" of mammary glands is characteristic of all mammals and it is not at all rare for humans of either sex to have supernumerary, or extra, nipples.

The basic mammary structure is present but undeveloped in males and tends to enlarge slightly during infancy, at puberty and in old age. Boy and girl babies sometimes have a slight secretion from the nipples that used to be called "witch's milk." This secretion is thought to be stimulated by the mother's hormones and disappears after a few weeks.

Gynecomastia—enlarged breasts in males—can be caused by some diseases and also by certain drugs, including digitalis, marijuana, heroin and alcohol, all of which stimulate estrogen production in males and diminish sperm count.

Another theory suggests that nipples, being erogenous zones, are present in males to encourage hugging behavior. To carry on our Chevy notion, we can view male nipples as the blanks in the dashboard where the stereo and air-conditioner would have gone if you'd ordered them from the factory.

BETWEEN THE ACTS

Q: I am an avid reader of novels of all types and quality. Without exception, in absolutely every heterosexual sex scene, the female half goes into the bathroom for a few minutes before sex commences. My question: What does she do in there? Allow me to add that I myself am both female and sexually active. Nevertheless, I am mystified by this apparently universal (except for me) practice. Are they all shy diaphragm users? Do they all have to pee? Are they washing their crotches?

— *A Faithful Reader and Typical American*

A: The Slicer generally avoids such topics, but from time to time, a question of such universal curiosity arises....

As The Slicer recalls, Selena, in the original *Peyton Place*, did not resort to any offstage preludes. In other novels it seems to be a mere suspense-building device to heighten anticipation, though whether it's a trick used by the depicted female or the author does vary. The Slicer conducted an informal opinion poll of 109 of Portland's literate females between the ages of 21 and 76, asking their opinions of what goes on in those fictional bathrooms. The results were as follows: washing, 90 percent; peeing, 60 percent; inserting diaphragm, 70 percent. More than 60 percent said "all of the above." A cantankerous 4 percent replied "praying." When queried, a statuesque 76-year-old looked down her aristocratic snoot and said,"If you don't know, my dear, you shouldn't be in that position."

An erudite historian, inspired by the question and adamant in her vote for the diaphragm, pointed out that the ancient Egyptians experimented with diaphragmatic equivalents. She also noted that the rakish Lord Byron was known to present his mistresses with a solid gold sphere, two inches in diameter and stamped with his crest. The sphere was meant to serve the purpose of a diaphragm. Byron being no piker, the women were allowed to keep the memento when his passions drifted to other climes.

LIMP STICKS

Q: My year in Vietnam left me free of any effects from Agent Orange, and I'm thankful. However, I'm seriously considering a lawsuit against the Air Force because of another chemical.

When I was in basic training in 1954, our food was laced with saltpeter to curb our sex drive. Anyone in our outfit who stayed up late and who wasn't deaf will tell you that it didn't work on me.

Well, after a 28-year military career and three years into retirement, it is just now starting to work! Can you recommend a good middle-aged female lawyer to help me with this problem?
— *Speaking Louder and Carrying a Soft Stick*

A: "Soft Stick" should consult a doctor before starting in on the lawyer search. The tale of saltpeter in boot camp, prison and high school cafeteria foods has been around for a long time. The Slicer consulted the Pentagon for starters. The Pentagon was less than eager to be consulted and kept shunting the question to various Veterans Administration offices in Washington, D.C. Eventually, however, Susan Hansen, public affairs officer for the Directorate for Defense Information, finally came through with a formula denial that saltpeter was introduced to the food of any military personnel from World War II to the present. "We have found no evidence of such a policy," says Hansen. This is America, of course, and that was the Pentagon, so The Slicer turned to the erudite James Achenbach in the media department at Oregon Health Sciences University. Achenbach interviewed several doctors on the subject, and, though none of them would go on the record, not one of them believes that saltpeter has any effect on the human libido. An expert on male sexual dysfunction told Achenbach, "I know of no scientific studies documenting the effect of saltpeter on libido." This confirms the opinions of two urologists who would talk with The Slicer as long as their names weren't mentioned (come on, guys, why is this such a tender topic?). They don't believe that saltpeter diminishes sexual urges or functions.

Interestingly, a muckamuck at the VA—who didn't want his name used—called the whole myth a "snipe hunt" perpetrated by drill sergeants to frighten and subdue the recruits. You can see how it would work—brainwashing depends on the suggestibility of humans. Cut their hair off, take away their constitutional rights, then tell them you've got their balls as well and they'll probably believe you.

SILVER SHOCK

Q: Why does people's hair turn gray when they get older? Is gray hair really gray or just white strands mixed in with pigmented strands? Why don't animals have gray hair? Or do they? Can a person's hair really turn white overnight if they get a severe emotional or physical shock?

— *Bewildered Brunette*

A: Dr. Frank Parker, chairman of the Department of Dermatology at the Oregon Health Sciences University, answered this for us. Yes, gray hair is gray or white. It is what you see if the pigment cells in the hair follicles stop producing pigment—just light shining through the translucent shaft of hair. And it happens to skin all over the body, not just hair. That's why our skin tends to get blotchy as we age.

Animals definitely go gray or white if they live long enough, and, yes, a very severe shock can, over a short period of time—several days or a few weeks—cause large numbers of pigment cells to give up the ghost. The condition, called vitiligo, causes hair loss and blotches of white in the skin and the remaining hair. Though the hair does grow back—usually white—the color does not. There is a theory, according to Dr. Parker, that all graying of hair is a form of vitiligo—which does *not* prove, he says, that our beloved former President Reagan has never endured a shock in his life, because some folks are genetically equipped to get very old without graying.

POPEYE SYNDROME

Q: As a kid I frequently heard the story of a woman who, upon seeing a car roll over her child, lifted the car with no mechanical help in an attempt to rescue her child. Apparently the cause of her superhuman strength was a massive rush of adrenaline. Any truth to this?

— *Waiting With Bated Breath in NE*

A: There are a thousand variations on this crisis-strength story, and, if humans do it, it isn't "superhuman." The Slicer talked with Dr. William Toffler, director of the Family Practice Clinic, on this subject because of his special interest in exercise and strength. Toffler says people who are not used to performing to the limit of their abilities may, with "maximal motivational stimulus do as much as their muscle-tendon system is capable of." People do astounding things under such circumstances—a 90-pound guy who wouldn't normally lift the economy-size detergent by himself might shift a few hundred pounds in a crisis.

As for cars, a healthy, desperate adult might briefly lift one corner if a jack slips and the other three wheels are on the ground. Toffler says that there is no documented proof of a human being ever lifting a ton. Cars generally range from one to two tons or more. World-class athletes, with genetic talents and years of training, sometimes, in the adrenal rush of competition, exert more force than their muscles, tendons or even bones can withstand, causing grisly injuries. But if a great heavyweight lifter hasn't been able to hoist a ton, neither has Mrs. McGillicuddy in a crunch.

PREGNANT WOMEN'S URINE & WEIGHT LOSS

Q: A fat guy where I work was told to lose 100 pounds or lose his job. He's actually lost about 75 pounds in the last six months and he says it's all done with injections of pregnant women's urine. He's pulling my leg, right?

— Chubby, Yes. Stupid, No.

A: He's pulling his own leg, but be a pal. Don't let him read this until he loses the last 25 pounds. The stuff he's probably talking about is a hormone extracted from the urine of pregnant women by a freeze-drying process. The hormone is called human chorionic gonadotropin (HCG for short), and it is produced by the human placenta.

Dave Chesney of the Food and Drug Administration says several studies were made, beginning a few years ago, to determine whether HCG is useful in treating obesity. One such study in Portland is currently winding down (or up) its results. Chesney explains that most of the other studies have ended and the FDA is eliminating approval for this research.

The results indicate conclusively that HCG does not work for losing weight. Ayerst Laboratories in New York markets HCG under the brand name APL. Current labeling requirements include a disclaimer to the effect that HCG is not effective in the treatment of obesity. It doesn't reduce hunger pangs. It doesn't burn calories faster. It does not flush fat away in the night, nor does it perform any of the other phantasmagorical things that we all wish *something* would perform.

HCG possesses a "gonad-stimulating" mechanism, according to Chesney, and is sometimes used for stimulating ovulation in infertile females or for correcting male hormone imbalances and their results —undescended testicles, for example.

Chesney assures us that the urine in question is not saved from the samples pregnant women submit to their health-care specialists during prenatal checkups. It is collected from paid donors.

That formerly fat guy may have dropped that chunk by the sheer power of belief in the shots. We do tend to place a great deal of credibility in anything we pay a lot for. Or maybe he discovered carrots. Or maybe his car broke down and he's been chasing buses. Whatever you do, don't tell him about HCG until he's finished his first 10K.

GILTY SECRETS

Q: Remember body paint, the all-over color-chic cosmetic? If I wear my favorite kiwi green to the Boo Ball on Halloween to pass for that Jolly Green Giantess, *Portlandia*, how big a patch of skin do I have to leave bare so as not to suffocate à la *Goldfinger*?
— *Costume Crazed*

A: The gilding-death scene in the movie *Goldfinger* spread one of the wildest myths far and wide. In fact the pores of the human skin don't breathe. They exude but they don't inhale. We get our air through our noses and mouths. We cannot suffocate by being completely covered with paint, mud, water, gilt or anything else unless the substance is toxic in itself and penetrates the skin to affect the bloodstream.

SEX CURE FOR HAY FEVER!

Q: It's that time of year again. Hay fever. Only two remedies offer relief—allergy medication and orgasm. One doesn't last long enough and the other leaves me tired. My question is this: Why does orgasm clear my sinuses?
— *Confused and Exhausted*

A: "Confused" neglects to specify which remedy is so exhausting. If it is allergy medication, "Confused" should ask a medical type about cortisone nasal spray or some of the new antihistamines that do not cause drowsiness.

A prominent allergy specialist (who does not wish to be named in conjunction with this question) says orgasm has no known effect on sinus congestion. "Confused" probably just "forgets about it for a while," says the expert.

Another equally anonymous specialist says it is vaguely possible that vigorous exercise and the attendant increase in circulation might help briefly. The effects have not been explored fully and wouldn't be much use in a severe allergy attack.

Q: The allergy specialist you consulted regarding the sinus-clearing virtues of orgasm either a) doesn't have hay fever or b) doesn't have orgasms. Any sexually active allergy sufferer can confirm "Confused and Exhausted's" observation that orgasm clears the sinuses; after all, the olfactory sense is a very important component of the sexual experience. The key is *adrenaline*.

Your allergy expert probably prescribes a shot of adrenaline as the antidote to the adverse reactions that sometimes follow allergy shots.

Like orgasm, other adrenaline producers, such as strenuous exercise and the ingestion of certain controlled substances also clear the sinuses. Like orgasm, unfortunately, their effects are short lived. Alas, the only true remedy for hay fever is to move to a home above the timber line and remain there from spring thaw to autumn frost.

— *D.B.*

THE SMOOCH: ITS USES AND ABUSES
Q: Where does kissing come from? Why do we do it?

— *Poontar*

A: Interestingly, this is one activity that is supposed to be strictly recreational. Ideally we do it simply because it feels good, never dutifully or for pay.

The act of kissing supposedly springs from that primordial mammalian impulse for nourishment and comfort: sucking.

Human infants also go through a nerve-racking phase in which their favorite way to investigate anything is to put it in their mouths. Infants who survive this dangerous compulsion are weaned onto the more discreet sipping of small tastes of the comforting flesh of their friends.

Mouth-to-mouth kissing is another matter. Far from universal, the practice is unknown in most primitive cultures and in much of Asia. This caress is popular throughout the Western world and in India, as evidenced by the Kamasutra.

Modern anti-osculates claim that the kiss was discovered by barbarians invading Rome (the Visigoths, not the Sun Bow Tours bus), who found they could use their mouths as a gag to stifle screaming by rape victims, while leaving their hands free for molestation.

A local osculation enthusiast whose first love is barley and hops claims that M-to-M kissing is a memorial to the last ounce of Jameson's Irish left on the Ark. The last swallow, says this expert, was shared lovingly by Noah and his wife by passing it from mouth to mouth, never swallowing, until the liquid fire was completely absorbed by the membranes of their mouths. This act of generous friendship, claims our pal, has been commemorated endlessly in the back seats of buckboards and Buicks ever since.

Scholar Nicolas J. Perella devoted years to his history of kiss symbolism in religion and art, titled *The Kiss Sacred and Profane* (University of California Press, 1969). Perella points out a pervasive theme of "eating" or seeking to absorb into oneself things seen as good or beautiful. Citing the 1897 writings of a French anthropologist, Perella points out that "the Chinese felt a kind of horror, as at some cannibalistic act, when confronted with the Western custom of mouth-to-mouth kissing."

Perella's own view is that the tradition grew out of early notions of the breath as the spirit or soul. The mingling of breaths was seen as the blending and joining of spirits. The nose-rubbing cultures, which extend from the Yukon to the Trobriand Islands and beyond, also are mingling their breath spirits. All this does lend a certain urgent mystique to the mint and mouthwash industries.

WHY SCREECHES HURT

Q: Why does the sound of fingernails scraping a chalkboard, or rubbing [two pieces of] Styrofoam together, bother some folks and not others?

—J.B.

A: Some folks are deaf to high-pitched sounds. Some folks have higher pain thresholds than others. One characteristic biologists use to tell the difference between living things and rocks is the ability to respond to outside stimulus. This responsiveness is called "irritability." One could say that the more irritable the creature, the more alive it is. This leads us to the third theory, which explains why some people are insensitive clods.

Sue Doucette, M.S., a clinical audiologist interning at Good Samaritan Hospital, insists on putting the thing more generously. The resonance chambers of the human ear vary, even in individuals with normal hearing. Of course, the human ear is not capable of hearing all the sound around it. Our best hearing range is the same as the speaking range of the human voice: from 250 cycles per second, a.k.a. hertz, to 2,000 or 4,000 hertz. Doucette says our ear actually amplifies the volume of higher pitches in the range so that things such as screaming babies and screeching Styrofoam can be excruciating.

The Slicer has noticed that the person who makes the noise rarely is as perturbed by it as are those listening. Whether it's fireworks, fingernails, shrieks or explosions, the guy causing the ruckus may delight in sounds that have the audience fleeing for sanity. This is often noticeable at rock concerts.

THAT MOST DREADED PLAGUE—THE YAWN

Q: Why are yawns contagious?

— *The Southeast Portland After-Dinner Slicer Fan Club and Question Factory*

A: Nobody knows. Dr. John Walker at Good Samaritan Hospital's Cognitive Neuropsychology Laboratory agrees that yawns are contagious but says this fascinating phenomenon is hard to study. Walker explains that yawning deliberately to elicit a yawn from someone else may work once or twice but not consistently. The impulse can be overridden. Experimental subjects can simply refuse to go along.

Madalene Anderson, nurse practitioner with the Regional Sleep Disorders Clinic at Good Sam, says that there is very little literature on the yawn and that the cause of the contagion is unknown.

Yawning in general is a primitive autonomic reflex. Some speculate that the contagion is a conditioned response. Anderson says that the contagion is most pronounced when people are bored or tired and that even babies are known to be susceptible.

Walker recalls the theory that yawning is somehow connected to the habit in some primates of opening their mouths wide and baring their teeth at one other. Walker says he doesn't hold to this theory at all.

The physiological function of the yawn is to open the collapsed alveoli in the lungs, expanding the volume of available air. Sighs work the same way but less dramatically. Another function of the yawn, familiar to us all, is to "pop" our ears, that is, to equalize the air pressure in our inner ear with the surrounding atmosphere by briefly opening the Eustachian tubes. This is useful in airplanes as well as in the express elevators to the 30th floor of Big Pink.

Dr. Gideon Bosker, an emergency room specialist as well as a writer, points out that yawning is one symptom of deterioration in the condition of a patient with a severe head injury. This specialist also theorizes that yawning may not actually be contagious but may be evidence of several individuals reacting to the same stress, boredom, fatigue or lack of oxygen. This speculator also considers the human inclination to mimicry: "We are walking apes. If someone has a rash on his face, people talking to him will often scratch themselves in the same spot...."

Why do people watch X-rated movies? Maybe all human activity is contagious."

For the record, The Slicer yawned compulsively throughout this research and found everyone consulted on the subject also inclined to yawn.

SPRING FEVER AND ITS OFFSPRING

Q: Sitting outside in the blooming fuchsia garden of our favorite locale (L'Auberge), in our favorite time of year (spring), imbibing our favorite tonic (red wine) and discussing our favorite subject (sex), we were wondering if there is any correlation between the heightened sex drive and activity (or is there any?) at this time of year (spring fever) and pregnancy (December births).

The real question: Is there any one month with more births than the other months? And what about an astrological sign with the most people?

— Spring Fever Hit Hard

A: Not in Oregon. Not recently. The kindness of Joyce Grant-Worley, statistics researcher for the Oregon Health Division, provides these numbers for 1986 and 1988.This is the way they break down per month:

	1986	1988
January	3,086	3,092
February	2,865	3,173
March	3,299	3,448
April	3,375	3,510
May	3,544	3,670
June	3,339	3,534
July	3,495	3,677
August	3,462	3,608
September	3,361	3,552
October	3,115	3,493
November	2,849	3,153
December	3,060	3,435
Total births	38,850	41,345

There is not an enormous variation, although, possibly, with December, January and February on the medium to low end of the birth rate, these figures could suggest a slightly lower incidence of impregnation in the spring. The total number of abortions in 1988 in Oregon was 13,309, but this figure isn't broken down by month. *Homo sapiens* are notoriously human for all seasons. But then Oregon has an equable climate with a steady food supply and widespread awareness of birth control measures. The Slicer wouldn't presume, on the basis of statistics from this neck of the woods, to eliminate the possibility of varying birthrates elsewhere.

SWITCHING SEXES

Q: There have been a number of sex-change operations from male to female, but I'm not aware of any women becoming men. Have there been any? Any ideas why so few women want to be men?

— *Pondering in Forest Grove*

A: The Slicer can think of many physical and cultural reasons for gratitude at not having been born male. Males are subject to the draft and are far more likely to be assaulted or murdered than females. Males are capable of fewer orgasms, and their clothes are lamentably dowdy. Although males have traditionally dominated the power spheres, they also get blamed for everything that goes wrong. It looks like a mighty rough row to hoe.

Nonetheless, just as many women want to become men as vice versa. Judy van Maasdam, director of the Palo Alto-based Harry Benjamin International Society for Gender Dysphoria, says the numbers are 50-50. The older literature on the subject claimed that there were four or five males actively seeking to become female for every female seeking to become male. Traditionally, subtracting a penis and testicles and creating a vagina was surgically simpler than the additive process required to create a phallus and appurtenances. The female-to-male process still involves more complex surgery, but, van Maasdam explains, recent advances in technique have made the transformation available to many more people. Although there is no centralized documentation of the numbers of such surgeries, van Maasdam agrees with other authorities who estimate that 400 to 500 transsexual operations are performed in the United States each year.

Psychiatrist Dr. Geoffrey Hyde, formerly of Portland and now practicing in Bend, works with several transsexual patients and has studied gender-dysphoria syndrome, as this discomfort with one's original anatomical gender is called. Hyde says there are 10 to 12 such surgical transformations per year in Oregon.

Candidates for transsexual surgery usually undergo extensive counseling in advance and live as their chosen gender for a year prior to surgery. Presurgical hormone treatments help induce some biological changes such as beard production for women becoming men and mammary enlargement for men becoming women.

FLAMING FLATULENCE

Q: Have you ever seen anyone light a fart? Techniques to prevent assburn? Color of lit-fart flame?

— X,Y & Z

A: The Slicer has never been privy to this arcane mystery and has always been curious about it. Colloquial references to the ritual crop up frequently but, as with the secret initiation ceremonies of various fraternal organizations and other tribal societies, seldom in detail. Thought to be an exclusively male rite (though contradictory information would be received with interest), the practice is widespread with devotees and dilettantes on at least four continents.

The Slicer's anonymous sources agree that the flame, in keeping with the high methane content of the expelled gas, is blue with a yellow streak or center.

The rite is usually performed in groups, and often during the ingestion of alcohol, which is said to contribute to impressive flatulence—and to the willingness to demonstrate.

The classic form is a team effort as follows: One guy jumps up, pulls down his pants and bends over, exposing his posterior to a flame bearer. The man with the flame holds the match or cigarette lighter close to the sphincter. The gas passes across the flame, igniting as it goes. A narrow margin of error is involved in being close enough to get a concentrated jet of gas without scorching the stern. The result is observed closely by the audience and either applauded or critiqued. Apparently, the ritual plays a role in establishing standing within the social hierarchy, but its exact significance remains obscure.

Variations have been reported, in which the underpants remain in place —the gas passing through the fabric. Another version has both expelling and lighting performed by the same person, clothed or naked, in a seated position with legs spread and the flame held in front of the crotch. Both sources warn that thin cotton underclothing is the only kind to wear for these versions. Nylon or other synthetics may not allow the gas to escape, creating a flammable cloud inside the shorts with the danger of ignition inside the garment. The resulting burns might offer diversion to the emergency room physician in attendance but are otherwise undesirable. Most sources say that backflash is not generally a problem in the classic form.

Initiates inform us that the practice has benefited greatly from the introduction of one-flick lighters. The old days of the wooden match required careful timing to avoid being left flameless at the critical instant.

The question of the antiquity of the practice is puzzling. Flint and steel would have been awkward and unreliable fire makers. One can, however, visualize a candle or, in ruder times, a small firebrand being pressed into service.

Poet and essayist, Doug Marx, a collector of Skid Road folklore, offers the ancient "Six Kinds of Farts" chant from his archives: "A Fuzz, a Fizz, a Fuzzy Fizz, a Ripsnort, a Tearass and a Poo." The first three, Marx explains, are onomatopoetic; the next two are high-velocity forms with a tendency to blow out the match. Marx describes the Poo as "the vilest of all," a covert weapon—rancid and silent, an expanding cloud without velocity—so stealthy that its source cannot be identified.

Somewhere, The Slicer hopes, there are Ph.D. candidates dedicated to recording and analyzing these oral—and anal—traditions.

FUR VS HAIR

Q: So. My boyfriend and I were lying in the sack, after you-know-what, and—attempting to compliment him, you understand—I told him he was nicely furred. He, being an argumentative sort, told me that people don't have fur. Only hair, says he. I told him that we have both: Hair keeps growing, while fur grows to a certain length, then stops. Therefore, the growth in the, ahem, nether regions is fur. The growth upon the noggin is hair. I'm not sure about the armpits, being that I've always shaved mine.

Which is all by the way of asking, O Noble Slicer, what's the diff between hair and fur?

— *Concerned Citizen*

A: We call it fur when it's thick and on somebody we call an animal. If it's sparse, as on a pig or a rhino, we call it bristles. It's all hair. And all hair, including the stuff on the average human head, has a limited life span and a preordained maximum length. Most head hair falls out and is replaced after four years. Head hair does not have unlimited growth. Most "European" (that's how The Slicer's encyclopedia labels possessors of mildly wavy hair) males' hair won't get much longer than two feet. Most European women's hair stops growing at about three feet. There are, of course, exceptions, with growths of six or even eight feet of hair. The possibilities for each individual are a matter of DNA dictates.

Hair is wild stuff with many functions. Eyelashes, those handy dust screens and flirtation devices, have a life span of about 50 days. Some hairs function as tactile sense organs, as in cat whiskers. The thick, downy undercoat popular among minks and other quadrupeds serves as an insulating layer, commonly punctuated by coarse cover hairs that shed water and resist stains. Human head hair is similar to a horse's mane or the mane of a male lion. Theory has it that all hair evolved from mutant feathers.

2 Etiquette: Doing the Right Thing

WET SMOOCH

Q: I went swimming with my boyfriend in a public pool and the lifeguard told us to "cool it," meaning to stop kissing. I'm 23 and he's 30 and being reprimanded like children is infuriating, to say the least. Where do our rights stand in regards to public display of affection? Can somebody tell us to quit kissing or can we tell them to kiss off?

— *Affectionately, L.C.*

A: Anybody can tell you to quit kissing and you can tell anybody to kiss off. What happens after that varies, depending on where you are and a few other factors.

Ross Walker, director of communications for the Portland Bureau of Parks and Recreation, says there is no bureau policy forbidding kissing in pools, and Walker has never had any complaints about it.

An informal survey of several lifeguards on duty in Parks Bureau pools revealed general agreement. As one pool staffer put it, during an adults-only swim time guards view kissing as "no big deal, unless there's a lot of fondling and intimacy involved." If things get carried away they probably will ask you to save it for a more private situation. During recreational times for all ages, however, though the lifeguards will not be disturbed by a simple smooch or two, they will be quicker to ask you to desist. Lifeguards do this because other swimmers may be offended or made uncomfortable by public display. Rather than speak to the kissers, the offended probably will complain to the lifeguards, whose job it is to smooth everybody's feathers.

Stevie Remington, executive director of the Oregon chapter of the American Civil Liberties Union, points out that a private association, be it the Y or the MAC club or a hotel with a pool, could make such a rule if it wished and could forbid you access to the pool if you defied it.

A request that you cool it so as not to offend other swimmers is a different matter from telling you that kissing violates a pool rule.

An old saw claims that your right to swing your fist stops just short of the other guy's nose. What should concern L.C. is not legal rights but simple consideration for the comfort of all those people she is not kissing. Who knows what agony she may have inflicted on the lonesome and celibate, much less on the rigid and puritanical. For some bystanders, "L.C.'s" delight may have looked like a ham-on-rye in Mecca. For others it might have been like driving an ice-cream truck through Ethiopia at 60 mph. Another old saw says, "If you can't share it, keep it to yourself."

CORRECT CLAPPING

Q: To enlighten myself and the rest of the performing arts audience in this fair city, when is applause appropriate at a performance and when is it really disruptive?

We know that during jazz concerts and rodeos the audience

should respond to a nicely performed or familiar act with a little recognition in the form of applause. In the latter we could raise that to include whistles and yelps of joy. But in the concert hall, in the theater and at the ballet is that behavior boorish and rude? Is the applause really best saved for the end, not just a pause, of a piece?

Should we control ourselves for a little while? Hold the whistles and foot stomping and save them for the parking lot afterwards or take them to a Blazer game where the other fans appreciate it? Please straighten all of this out so I can know if I should bring my compressed-air horn to the next symphony concert.

— *A Patron of the Arts Who Had the Misfortune of Sitting Next to a Cretin Who Applauded Every 20 Seconds During Act II of* Swan Lake *Last Saturday*

A: The Slicer feels that a primary drawback of many cultural events is the scarcity of air horns, stomping and whooping. This belief ensures that The Slicer attends far more boxing matches than concerts.

Enlisting the expertise of those better informed, The Slicer offers the following guidelines for cultured clapping.

A rule of thumb for any performance that has a curtain is when the curtain closes, applaud. When the houselights come up, stop applauding.

Dance critic, Martha Ullman West, says it is appropriate, during a dance performance, to applaud when the stars first come on stage. Stars may be recognized, West assures us, by their spotlights. Applause is also correct if the soloist does something outrageously spectacular, such as jumping higher than is humanly possible or twirling around 32 times on one toe without either falling down or throwing up.

Some, like The Slicer, are so desperately ignorant that everything on the stage seems astounding—beginning with how the women keep their long hair in those tidy buns while lolloping about so violently. We bemused should take our clapping cues from the more knowing audience members. The experts at the Schnitz, West explains, usually are concentrated in the first few rows of the dress circle or mezzanine level, "because the aficionados who can afford it want to get slightly above the stage so they can watch the floor patterns."

One applauds at the end of each act, if only in joy at escaping to the champagne in the lobby. The critical West insists also that one always applauds at the end because, no matter what you think of the performance, the dancers worked very hard indeed.

Civilized musical performances have their own code, for which we turn to classicist and music scholar, Larry Fuchsberg. In general, Mr. F. explains, one applauds at the end of the piece but not during the pause between movements. Everybody knows this, of course. What we don't know is how to tell when sudden silence is just a pause between movements.

The clues, says Fuchsberg, are discovered quickly. String quartet musicians usually will not lower their bows. The conductor of an orchestra doesn't turn to face the audience between movements. When the conductor turns to look our way, it's OK to clap.

Opera, on the other hand, can be tricky for the novice applauder. "Italian opera," explains Mr. F., "is often written to allow the audience to express appreciation after certain pieces." The singer usually tips off the crowd by freezing at the end of the song or stepping back slightly, out of character for an instant. "The script often calls for the aria to be followed by the singer making an exit. But if they're offstage they can't receive their applause. To remedy the problem, a technique is often used called 'the Vienna curtain call.'" It usually involves forgetting some prop and having to return for it. "For example," says Mr. F., "in the third act of The Marriage of Figaro, the count sings a rage aria and is meant to storm offstage at the end. The singer will often pretend to have forgotten something. An account book perhaps. This brings him back on stage to grab the book and, incidentally, to receive his applause."

Fuchsberg suggests that Portland audiences adopt the European practice of rhythmic clapping en masse to signal a desire for an encore or another curtain call. The steady rhythmic coercion is easier on the applauders' hands than normal helter-skelter clapping and sounds as though it can go on all night if the crowd's desires are thwarted.

West's request for audience etiquette is that if we *must* break the auditorium rules by sneaking our soda pop cans to our seats, we refrain from hurling them onto the stage at the final bows.

CHARGE-A-TIP

Q: Do waiters and waitresses prefer to be tipped in cash or on a charge card—assuming the amount is the same?

— *Ed B.*

A: Our sources say this is not a major problem at all, but several waiters and bartenders told The Slicer they generally prefer cash, even though their establishments let them trade in charged tips for cash at the end of their shifts. "The less of a paper trail we leave for the IRS," says one experienced booze slinger, "the better we like it."

DISCOVERING THE CORPSE

Q: Hypothetical situation: You are 19 years old. You have no immediate family save your grandmother, who lives with you and is ailing. One day you come home from work and your grandmother is dead. Whom do you call? The police? The funeral parlor? The hospital?

— *A. Jones*

A: Whether you're 9, 19 or 90, the answer is the same: 911. Dial it.

If you call a hospital, they'll probably tell you to call 911. If you call the funeral parlor, they may well tell you to call 911. A funeral parlor may end up making arrangements and necessary phone calls for you but will probably charge you for the service.

This is a case of "unattended death," meaning that death

took place outside a hospital and not in the presence or care of a medical practitioner. In such cases it is always important to determine the cause of death to prevent murder from going undetected.

The 911 dispatchers will send police and any necessary medical help. The police will call the county medical examiner. If the deceased was terminally ill and under the care of a physician who is willing to confirm the cause of death and sign a death certificate, the medical examiner can give the police the right to release the body so that it can be taken to a mortuary. The police will help make the arrangements.

Terry Sparks, the deputy medical examiner for Multnomah County, explains that if there is no physician in a position to sign the death certificate or if there is anything questionable about the circumstances, his office will send a representative to the scene. The medical examiner will either release the body to a funeral home or pick up the body and perform an autopsy before releasing it to relatives.

If an M.D. is in attendance at the death, you can phone the county medical examiner (248-3746 for Multnomah County) directly and forget about 911.

A FORK IN THE ROAD

Q: We all know that Europeans use their dinner cutlery differently from Americans. They hold their knife in the right hand and the fork, tines toward the plate, in their left, conveying food to the mouth in a most efficient way. Americans laboriously cut off a morsel, put down the knife and switch the fork to the right hand for conveying food with the tines facing up. What I want to know is why? When did the difference come about?

— *Not Critical but Curious*

A: Several readers have asked about this over the years. Haunted by the question, The Slicer has nosed unavailingly through dozens of etiquette books and asked several folk who are known for not dribbling at the table. No luck. Desperate, The Slicer appealed to the viewers of the ill-fated and now defunct *2 at Four* program on KATU. To all those who responded by phone and mail, thanks.

Doreen King of Portland, for example, asked her cousin Betty (Elizabeth Sharples) in Lancashire, England. Cousin Betty pointed out that the fork was unknown in England until the reign of James I (about 1603), when the implement arrived from Italy. People ate with a knife in their right hand aided by the fingers of their left hand.

Natasia Chan, corroborated by her Cleveland High history teacher, Mrs. Ireland, proposes that the American technique was adopted to demonstrate opposition to the British during the Revolutionary War.

Steven Peterkort of Portland wrote, "Miss Manners says in her book that the American method is superior because it is more complicated and impractical and thus a more advanced form of social behavior (pp. 123-125, *Miss Manners' Guide to Excruciatingly Correct Behavior*, Atheneum, 1982)."

A helpful type in the *Oregonian*'s newsroom provided The Slicer with the New York phone number of the United Media Features Syndicate, which distributes the Miss Manners column. The divine Miss M. was in Maine, explained her representative, Joan Slack, but when she returned Joan would ask her. Joan called back this week. Miss Manners says the American method is the old European aristocrats' way. It was the Europeans who changed back to the peasant technique. She doesn't know when the change came about or why.

Here is The Slicer's completely unsubstantiated theory. When forks drifted in, only the aristocracy could afford them. The cumbersome, inefficient technique displayed the cutlery and demonstrated that the rich weren't ravenous even at dinner time. Then came the French Revolution. Monsieur Guillotine was poised and hungry for aristocrats. Suddenly it wasn't cool to appear more hoity-toity than Madame Defarge. Those who could afford forks reverted to the poor folks' method of shoveling the grub in as quickly as possible. The French were, even then, trendsetters and soon convinced the rest of Europe that this was the haute technique. Voilà! Executioner's etiquette.

GONZO GADFLY

Q: Why are all journalists, whether print or broadcast employed, so eager to destroy the best efforts of our leaders in government? You can't all be communists, can you?

— Tired of Negativism and Publicized Security Leaks

A: The Slicer likes to think journalists would be just as critical whether Mother Theresa, Fidel Castro or Bud Clark were running the world. A Midwestern university conducted several years' worth of research to distinguish between inherited and environmentally determined characteristics in humans. The findings suggested that verbal ability is an inherited trait inextricably linked to another trait: attitude toward authority. The two traits occur, evidently, in inverse proportions. The greater your verbal ability, the more negative your attitude toward authority. This translates into the fortune cookie motto, "If you can talk, bitch." Genetic engineering will soon make it possible to ensure that whole populations are docile, reverent, obedient and mum. Until then, The Slicer figures that anytime a nosy cub reporter fresh from journalism school can pick up a top-secret tidbit, the KGB could probably do the same, so our so-called security system is about as substantial as my grandmother's hairnet. The most embarrassing item to emerge in the last few decades has to be the CIA list of its *attempted* assassinations that failed. No wonder they wanted to hire a more efficient outfit like the Mafia.

CROSSING OVER

Q: I've seen your column in the Willamette Week for a while. It appears no subject is too outrageous for you to respond to. So, for my interest and that of your readers, I'd like to put a question to you and see what response I (and likely, you) get. What would be the possibility of a male cross-dresser having a serious relationship with you? (If in doubt, a male cross-dresser is a man who feels comfortable and sexy in women's clothes.)

—*Kira LaRosa*

A: Many topics are too outrageous for this columnist to respond to: restaurant questions, anything more to do with either the Banfield or I-5 and much more. You should know, however, that there is only room for one "serious relationship" in The Slicer's life, and that slot is occupied by a profoundly emotional entanglement with the Internal Revenue Service. My auditor, of course, may be a cross-dresser, but I see him only in his ash-gray uniform, never in civvies. He has me booked solid for the next 35 years.

EMPTY HANDED

Q: What are my rights when stopped for shoplifting? When I was stopped I cooperated short of emptying my pockets and suggested the shop owner call the police. He did. The officer searched me and found nothing. Do I have recourse for that embarrassment and invasion of privacy? What is appropriate etiquette for that situation?

—*Felix*

A: The Slicer is not qualified to offer legal advice, and in any case Felix has not provided enough details from this incident for even a lawyer to know whether a civil suit could be brought.

Because we are approaching the beginning of the shoplifting season, which peaks (according to the Oregon Law Enforcement Council) in December and March, some general guidelines may be useful.

Steve Wax, the federal public defender for Portland, says, "In general a suspect's basic rights are the same whether the crime is shoplifting or murder." You have the right to remain silent. You are under no obligation to provide information to anyone.

If you have not formally been arrested you have the right to refuse a search. If a police officer just says, "Hey, let me take a look in your knapsack," you can say yes or no as you please. If you have been placed under arrest, the officer may and probably will search you without a warrant. Wax warns that these are general rights.

As for Felix's situation, lawyer Forrest N. Rieke of Rieke Geil & Savage points out that the two main questions in Felix's letter concern the search itself and being stopped at all. "Number 1," says Rieke, "he consented to the search, which affects the etiquette of the situation. Since he consented, he's not in a position to complain." Rieke explains that there might possibly, maybe, be grounds for a suit if the questioning took place in a public setting rather than in a private place, providing the merchant didn't have sufficient "probable cause" for detaining Felix.

WRITERS RIPPED OFF

Q: As an unpublished poet, I saw an ad for a World of Poetry contest in a popular magazine. I sent in a poem and was told later I won an Honorable Mention in the Great American Poetry Contest. Still later I was told I won their Golden Poet Award of 1987. So what's the problem, you ask? It seems they are only interested in getting money out of me. So I have concerns about their reputation. Who are they, and was I
—*Honored?*

A: Legal scams. Non-prosecutable con games. The Slicer's sources aren't familiar with this particular outfit, but be warned! There are a lot of grifters out there preying on the frustrations of aspiring writers.

So, it may not be an actual contest. Maybe the folks in charge don't care how good or lousy the poems are. Maybe all those who send in their five-buck entry fee get a letter saying they've won an Honorable Mention and their poem will appear in the soon-to-be-published volume; order form enclosed, send check or money order addressed to... Just maybe the only poems that appear are by people who happened to pre-order their copies of the "beautifully bound limited edition." Maybe, too, extra money is asked of those who get "special recognition" of some kind. When enough of those checks come in, a beautifully bound volume may actually be printed. Sometimes the poems are crammed five or ten to a page in micro-type. In any case the odds are that the only other people who ever read the thing will be the other folks who unwittingly bought their way into it. That may be hundreds or even thousands of people across the country, and it can be argued that it's more people than read the average poetry publication, but this sort of operation is not considered a legitimate publishing credit and won't add any luster to your résumé.

There are similar operations advertised for songwriters ("Your words set to music") where a studio cranks out a 45-rpm record or a three-minute cassette of your lyric set to supermarket Muzak or worse.

The great series of Who's Who imitations strikes The Slicer as being on the same lines (*Who's Who in Canine Proctology*, etc.). The way most poets, and fiction writers, get published is to hike down to the largest available magazine rack and jot down the addresses and editors' names of legit literary magazines. Send off your stuff with a stamped, self-addressed envelope and a brief introductory letter. Then sit back and collect rejection slips like everybody else. Every time the stuff comes back, send it out again to somebody else. The rejections aren't much fun, but when a piece gets picked up, it's because some editor, brute or booby though he may be, actually liked it.

3 Government Intervention

DEATH AND TAXES

Q: As Oregon chairman of the Victims for Capital Punishment (VCP), I'm writing in hopes that you will inform your readers of our efforts to introduce and pass legislation requiring the death penalty for convicted dealers of "hard" drugs....

— *VCP*

A: With all due respect for VCP's good intentions, they can buy an ad if they want to get their address out. The Slicer thinks capital punishment is a ludicrous boondoggle that has never worked. It doesn't deter crime. It doesn't cost less than lifelong boarding of hard-core thugs in penal seclusion. It doesn't allow the community as a whole to get its hostile rocks off at the bad guys. If the mom, dad or wife of a murder victim wants to walk up to the killer with a .44 and blow him away, The Slicer will holler Not Guilty, but these governmental executions go against the grain.

Furthermore, this whole "war on drugs" is doomed idiocy. You'd think the bluenoses of this nation would remember the message of Prohibition. The legal ban on alcohol managed to get a lot of folks killed and to create several enormous fortunes. The current approach to the drug problem is having the same effect. Oh, yeah, it also keeps a lot of law enforcement types off the unemployment roles.

Decriminalizing drugs and controlling their manufacture and distribution would eliminate an enormous chunk of the crime in this country and provide a hefty income in taxes that now are uncollectible. Certainly some percentage of the population would turn into vegetable mush just as they do on alcohol. But supporting the parasites would cost less and have less destructive impact on the community than the current crop of burglaries, muggings, stickups and murders.

DEATH REVISITED

Q: Re: June 4 "The Slice"…This time you've "sliced" off the "fairway"! When discussing the death penalty, it is too easy to confuse the "map" (what we'd all like in our ideal world) and the "territory" (what the real world is). The voters are not fooled—85 percent know what's real. Since The Slicer has been misled by idealists who only see the map, please allow me to expose you to the territory. No executed murderer has ever killed again—hence capital punishment is *not* a "ludicrous boondoggle." To the contrary, "life in prison" is the ludicrous boondoggle. The lifer murders guards, murders some poor guy in for three to five for his first offense, gets out by escaping or leave. (If you think I'm joking, I can cite specific examples, but the one that really stands out is our own Oregonian Marquette, who chopped up a lady in pieces, went to prison for "life," then got out and chopped up two more before he was caught!) The only time capital punishment costs more than life in prison is when "life" doesn't really mean life and when the people who confuse the map with the territory run up the cost of a murder trial with endless technical appeals.

What you should know that the map freaks don't want you to know is that the probability of a white male being murdered is about 1 in 168; the odds for a black male are "only" 1 in 28! So when the map freaks complain about the imbalance on death row, remind them that the great preponderance of murders are *not* interracial; hence, the map freaks are dooming the good hard-working majority of the disadvantaged to being preyed upon by their misguided brothers!

— *C.N.W.*

A: Hold your water, there, Bucky! The Slicer didn't bring up the issue of race and capital punishment, but as long as we're on it—according to demographer Everett Lee of the University of Georgia, as of January 1989, one out of every 20 (not 28) black men in the United States can expect to be murdered.

In the November '84 election, Oregon's vote for Ballot Measure 6 mandated a state constitutional amendment allowing the death penalty for the crime of aggravated murder. Ballot Measure 7, also passed in that election, specified that death be inflicted by lethal injection of an "ultrashort-acting barbiturate in combination with a chemical paralytic agent." Only crimes committed after the law went into effect in December 1984 are punishable by this law.

Aggravated murder is defined by ORS163.095 as murder occurring by contract; following a previous homicide conviction; of more than one victim; in the course of torture or maiming of a victim; by use of explosives; of any police, corrections or justice officers; of a juror or witness; or committed by a defendant while in custody.

Despite those crimes in which punitive revenge by *somebody* seems desirable, The Slicer, like many humans prone to temper tantrums and occasional irrational behavior, has always felt personally threatened by bureaucratic death penalties.

But just because The Slicer is flatly opposed to giving any government the power to inflict death on any of its citizens doesn't mean she's blind to the idiocy of letting the zipoids wander loose. Why do we never consider a revision of the appeal and sentencing procedures? If the death sentence were eliminated, the appeals process could be nipped considerably and a lot of taxpayers' moolah could be saved.

Or try using a little imagination! One reasonable alternative might be cryogenics, the freezing method that preserves organic items without damage. Freezing fetuses for future pregnancies is now becoming standard procedure. Soon they'll be able to flash-freeze capital criminals. Imagine how cheap it would be to store these thugsicles.... No guards. No food. No medical expenses. Just a refrigerator-repair crew for maintenance. The polar ice caps might be useful repositories, or, knowing how reluctant taxpayers are to ante up for jails, tax rebates could be offered to citizens volunteering storage space in their home freezers.

Consider, too, the possibility of future usefulness. Say you've got a brush fire war going in some distant and puny principality. You don't have to mobilize the pride of the nation and spend billions getting decent citizens smeared. You just decant a battalion of monsters. Or say the CIA needs an assassin. No need to incriminate government employees.... Why waste effective murderers with proven track records? Just pick an expert in the method desired—garrote, ice pick, plastic explosive or whatever—thaw him out and point him.

Those who resist the idea of conferring icy immortality on our worst cursed might prefer to sedate the critters until they die of old age or send them to Pluto with a sack lunch. The Slicer is willing to dicker within reason. Look what penal colonies did for Australia. Great movies. And the beer's good.

WHO'S BEEN HAD?

Q: The other night, nodding off in front of the 11 o'clock news, I could have sworn I heard about George Bush confessing to a sexual relationship with Ronald Reagan. None of my friends heard this, and they all think I'm nuts. I didn't see it splashed across the front page of *The Oregonian* the next day, nor even stitched in small print in the sports section. Have I gone gaga? And can I sue the news media for moral stress? Was I hallucinating?

—*Confused on Southeast Lambert*

A: The Slicer is not a lawyer, and "Confused" is not hallucinating. Though astrology in the Oval Office hogged most of that week's headlines, at least one TV network picked up the Bush item. During a campaign stop, Bush was asked to explain his relationship with the president. He answered, "We've had triumphs, we've had mistakes, and we've had sex." Recovering brillantly, the vice president denied having sex with Reagan, claiming he intended to say "setbacks."

A NEW DEAL FROM A NEW DECK
Q: Any Slicerian prognostications on who'll be in the running for Democratic presidential candidate in the next national election?

— *Already Dreaming*

A: Nope. The Slicer thinks we should redesign the whole elective process anyway. It's gone too far aglee. As things are, being willing to run for president is evidence that you're too deranged to handle the job. There ought to be some way to guarantee in our chief exec a minimum level of diplomatic skills, equanimity under fire and an acute awareness of the true nature and sentiment of the American public.

What if we altered the requisites for the office? Suppose we declare a lottery in which every four years we pull the name of our new president from a pool of all hard-liquor bartenders with at least 10 consecutive years' experience at the well. The only exemptions allowed would be for debilitating illness or possession of a degree in law.

LEGALIZE PROSTITUTION?
Q: Hey, Slice, cut the piffle for a minute and tell us, do you really think prostitution ought to be legalized?

— *Bewildered*

A: I haven't decided yet. Questions that have been around for 10,000 years sometimes take The Slicer a few months to figure out. I heard some new angles the other day from a big, friendly redhead who introduced herself as a union organizer for COYOTE (Call Off Your Old Tired Ethics), the prostitutes' rights organization. Her name is Carol Leigh (pronounced Lee).

"I'm also known as the Scarlet Harlot," she said, smiling. Leigh, 33, has been a practicing prostitute for six years. Far from hiding her profession from the police or the public, this San Francisco resident writes about it in poems, plays, stories and political tracts. She also does a Scarlet Harlot column for a Bay Area newspaper called *Appeal to Reason* and the Seattle monthly, *Northwest Passage*. Her acting skills, developed in classes paid for by prostitution, are frequently displayed in her one-woman stage comedy, *The Adventures of Scarlet Harlot, or the Demystification of Prostitution.*

Leigh is an advocate for prostitutes' rights. "You might call me a Presstitute," she jokes. "I seem to be doing more public relations work on this trip than actually talking with the prostitutes here for organizational purposes."

Leigh is not impressed with the Portland City Club report that recommended legalization of prostitution. In fact she was disgusted.

"They want to put us all on the street in an industrial zone," she complains. "That report is skeletal and misleading. They evidently did not talk with any prostitutes' rights groups at all. The City Club profile of a prostitute is a white 25-year-old. The average age of a prostitute in the United States is 19. They are only dealing with the street worker situation. At least 50 percent of Portland's prostitutes don't work the street at all. In most cities, only 15 to 20 percent are on the street. Most women work in massage parlors, escort services or through referral groups."

Leigh adds that "blacks are generally not allowed to work in the massage parlors. While 30 to 60 percent of the women on the street are women of color, 85 to 90 percent of those *sentenced* for prostitution are women of color. There's a dramatic racist element involved in enforcement."

All advocates of prostitutes' rights recommend decriminalization rather than legalization. Instead of creating a new body of laws to govern the trade, "decrim" simply lifts the laws against prostitution and allows it to be regulated by the same laws as other businesses.

COYOTE maintains that new laws for regulation, placed in the hands of government, perpetuate the stigma attached to sex work. The organization's platform points out that U.S. Department of Health statistics show only 3 to 8 percent of venereal disease in the United States to be related to prostitution and yet "compulsory health checks have historically been used to control and stigmatize prostitutes and not their customers." COYOTE opposes mandatory health checks while urging regular, voluntary checkups for men and women.

The real function of laws against prostitution, in Carol Leigh's view, is the social control of all women. "Consenting adults," she writes, "have the right to have sex with other consenting adults, and it is an infringement on our basic human rights for the law to tell us what we can and can't do in the bedroom."

How did a nice girl like Carol Leigh get into this trade? After graduating from Empire State University in New York and doing postgraduate work in literature at the University of Buffalo, Leigh aimed at a career in journalism. Instead she found herself slinging hash for a living. She didn't like it.

"I thought working in a massage parlor would be a great way to do an inside story on prostitution," she remembers. But after discovering that she could make $150 to $300 a night in San Francisco's Tenderloin district, she felt less than compelled to return to waiting on tables.

Leigh believes that sex work has been a liberating experience for her and that it serves a valuable purpose in society. While acknowledging that some prostitutes criticize her romantic view of a gritty and dangerous business, she is surprised that more women don't explore their sexuality through prostitution.

"Society sees prostitutes as victims, which is a way to see us as being punished for our sins," she maintains. Opposed to the submissively exploited role frequently depicted, Leigh views prostitution as a powerful political stance with a lot of bargaining moxie.

"Many women," she says, "feel pressured to give it away in return for security or affection. I feel I can't be owned because I own my own sexuality enough to sell it, to make choices about giving it away or not."

LAUNDERED MONEY

Q: What is "laundered money"? I have been washing clothes for over 50 years, and no one has ever asked me to wash their money. I just thought I might get rich in my old age if I could work up a list of clients who want their money laundered. Please rush reply via your column. I'm not getting any younger.

— *Seventy Years Old and Still Learning*

A: You might get rich but you risk having the feds interfere with your retirement plans. Laundering money is not a soap-and-water affair. It's a bookkeeping trick.

One of the sadder aspects of making your millions as a cocaine importer or as an impresario of illegal prostitution is that enjoying a lot of money is conspicuous. An anonymous phone call to the IRS from a cast-off sweetheart or an envious neighbor could trigger rude questions from implacable tax agents about how it is that a former parking lot attendant is suddenly paying cash for Ferraris, yachts and penthouse condos. The idea of laundering is to "filter" the dirty money; inventive accounting allows unseemly sums to surface in the guise of profits from a legitimate operation—a.k.a. the laundry.

Traditionally, a service or entertainment industry has made a better laundry than an enterprise that offers goods. The purchase and resale of widgets involves the preparation of revealing invoices and a lot of exposed links in a long chain. Say, however, that you have a little mud-wrestling club. If 50 people buy tickets at the door on any given night, what's to prevent you from tearing up 300 tickets? You show 300 ticket sales in your books, 250 of which are the share allotted by contract to your partner, Shifty McGoon. McGoon can now enter his share as income in his IRS forms. With a little digital dance on the old adding machine he can probably justify his conspicuous consumption. You and your mud-wrestling emporium get a cut of whatever you manage to launder.

This is a crude and strictly hypothetical example, of course. The laundry business can get pretty sophisticated. Who knows how many coins actually drop through the slots of the video games? Or how many condos in a "sold-out" high-rise are actually occupied?

Variations on the laundry are as old as those Siamese twins, crime and taxes, but it has been speculated that the modern forms were developed by bootleggers during Prohibition.

FABULOUS FIDEL

Q: My friends (e.g., Lorna, Bruce, Glenn) think I'm mad (or at least cognitively bent). You understand, I'm sure, that in the course of a social gathering one is sometimes tempted to toss out certain juicy little tidbits of information that reside in remote regions of the brain and are not likely to be supported by readily accessible written records. Recently, on one such occasion, I merely mentioned that Fidel Castro (the Cuban fellow) was a damned serious baseball player when he attended college here in the U.S, so serious, in fact, that he was forced to choose between playing pro ball and leading a revolution (apparently he chose the latter)! My friends were amused. I'm not crazy, am I? Was Fidel once a pretty fair ballplayer, or wasn't he?

— *Confused About Castro*

A: "Confused" isn't necessarily nuts, but has fallen for what is, apparently, an urban folk tale. Several enlightened types admit to having heard the story, often in the ironic form of Castro having tried out for the Washington Senators.

The downtown library's baseball encyclopedias show only

two Castros in the major leagues: William R. Castro of the Dominican Republic, a right-handed pitcher for the Milwaukee Brewers from '74 to '78, and Louis Castro, a second baseman for the Philadelphia Athletics in 1902. Though this doesn't eliminate the possibility of Fidel in college ball or the minors, his biographers—in four different books, by different authors with opposing political views—seem to scotch the idea. None of them mentions a North American sports connection and all maintain that Fidel was educated entirely in Cuba and took his law degree at the University of Havana. He did honeymoon for two weeks in Florida with his first wife, and he spent seven weeks traveling the United States on a fund-raising campaign before the revolution. On both trips, however, he seems to have focused on activities other than baseball. Nonetheless, Castro is a baseball fan. In his adolescence he talked his rich dad into buying the equipment for a teen team in his home village.

On the other hand, Fidel's son by his first marriage, Fidel Jr., a.k.a. Fidelito, was raised in this country. Could he be the source of this story?

For more intriguing urban folk tales, try the trilogy by collector Jan Brunvand: *The Vanishing Hitchhiker*, *The Choking Doberman* and *The Mexican Pet*.

ON THE RECORD

Q: For many years I've wondered how I could get hold of my FBI file. You seemed to be the perfect person to ask. I know that I have a file from civil-rights and anti-war protests. All I need is an address and I will write for it. Thank you.

—*Susan R.*

A: Remember, this is the feds, and nothing is ever as simple as just dropping them a polite note.

The central headquarters of the Federal Bureau of Investigation is reachable by mail at Justice/FBI, 9th Street and Pennsylvania Avenue, NW, Washington, D.C., 20535. Phone [202] 324-3691. The Washington central office will not search the files of any of its 49 field offices, so if you think one of the locals may have pertinent info you must write to it separately. The Justice Department does charge for Freedom of Information Act or Privacy Act record searches. The FOI/PA officer in the Portland office says copies of the first 180 pages of any record are free, but it's 10 cents a page after that. When writing, specify an amount you are willing to pay and ask them to notify you by phone before beginning a search that will cost more than that. You must also include enough personal information so the agency can identify you positively. State your full name, date and place of birth, and have your signature notarized. That's the absolute minimum. Some authorities say your Social Security number is required, but Portland's obliging FOI/PA officer says it's optional. Including copies of standard ID wouldn't hurt. You may also want to include any other names you've used, travel, other addresses, any government employment, political involvement, specific riots or sit-ins you've attended, and so on. You have to ask yourself, though, just how much of this you want the government to know.

It wouldn't hurt any of us to take a look at a copy of the Freedom of Information Act and the Privacy Act available at most libraries. An alternative is to save up pennies and send a check or a money order for $3 to the FOI Service Center, 800 18th Street, NW, Suite 300, Washington, D.C., 20006. Ask for a copy of the excellent publication *How to Use the Federal FOI Act*. Though the pamphlet is designed for use by journalists and scholars, it contains a fine general guide to both the Freedom of Information Act and the Privacy Act. You'll want to address the FBI under both acts to get the broadest coverage of data. The pamphlet also explains various snarls of exemptions and specific tactics for appeals and complaints.

The following is the "Sample Privacy Act Request Letter" provided in the copyright pamphlet:

Your address
Daytime phone number
Date

Privacy Act/FOI Act Office
Agency
Address
Privacy Act/FOI Act Request
Dear FOI/PA Officer:
Pursuant to both the Freedom of Information Act, 5 U.S.C./552, and the Privacy Act, 5 U.S.C./552a, I seek access to and copies of all records about me which you have in your possession.

To assist with your research for these records, I am providing the following additional information about myself: full name, Social Security number, date and place of birth (and any other personal data you don't mind revealing to the feds). If you determine that any portions of these documents are exempt under either of these statutes, I will expect you to release the non-exempt portions to me as the law requires. I, of course, reserve the right to appeal any decision to withhold information.

I promise to pay reasonable fees incurred in the copying of these documents up to the amount of $_____. If the estimated fees will be greater than that amount, please contact me by telephone before such expenses are incurred.

If you have any questions regarding this request, please contact me by telephone. Thank you for your assistance. I will look forward to receiving your prompt reply.
Very truly yours,
Signature
(You must have your signature notarized)
For help and advice on your requests you can call the FOI Service Center at [800] 336-4243.

4 Fashion Passions

SHINE ON

Q: What is the half-life of polyester?

— *Confirmed Natural Fiber Wearer*

A: Nine times around the golf course or twice around the shopping mall.

PIERCING

Q: It's happened several times now. A good-looking woman will be riding the same bus as myself, not surprising since there are many in Portland. Then I realize the woman has a stud earring on her left nostril. She has actually had her nose pierced! Being fairly easygoing about self-mutilation ('tain't my style but does me no harm), I thought little of the incidents. But only this month I saw a baby whose nose had been pierced.

That poor child had no choice and now must live with the results of her parents' vanity. Or are children being born with stud earrings in their noses? Or is it aliens from the stars whose only means of identifying each other is to appear normal except for a pierced nose? Or have I stumbled on yet another stupendous religious experience? Or...?

— *Curious George*

A: Piercing is definitely on the rise and there are more bizarro passions in the forked fetish we call humanity than are dreamed of in any one philosophy.

The Slicer's source for this information, a skilled piercer, prefers to remain anonymous so as not to be pestered with kinko requests.

These things are often culturally determined. Many European peoples traditionally pierce baby ears; many Eastern cultures have always pierced baby noses. The pierced nostril got its big boost in the United States in the '60s, when the fashion arrived with the Indian gurus. Even now, any college girl who goes to India is liable to come home with a pierced nostril because it's just so cool.

The ear-piercing establishments in the Portland Yellow Pages told The Slicer they do not pierce anything but ears, and they suspect that noses are being pierced at home by amateurs or by tattoo parlors.

Personally, The Slicer agrees that permanent body changes (including circumcision) should not be inflicted on children. As our "piercer" source adds, "One problem with piercing on a kid is that their face changes, their cranium grows, the skin moves upward and around. What starts as a pierced nose could end up on their ear." This is definitely true of tattooing children, which is part of the reason it is illegal in Portland to tattoo anyone under 18.

Please note that piercing of body parts has always been big in most parts of the world. The United States is peculiarly Calvinist and covert about such things. Fifteen years ago it was hard to find anyone in these parts who would pierce ears.

Now pierced fingernails are terribly chichi, and you might see a woman with a lip plug any day of the week.

Pierced nipples have long been considered a gay-male fashion, but the trend now includes heterosexuals, particularly women, and often couples.

The famous tattooed lady, Elizabeth Weinzirl, a doctor's wife now 85 years old, sports big gold rings through nipples she had pierced for her 75th birthday.

Pierced scrotal sacs and penises also have a certain vogue. That classic novel of humiliation, *The Story of O*, appeared in the '60s and intrigued a fair number of American and European women into piercing their labia, a fad that continues today.

Piercing and other body modifications such as stretching of ear lobes, lips, nipples and labia, along with the relatively sedate tattoo, seem to be gathering adherents in these parts. As our source informs us, "The wildest stuff is done by stodgy-looking lumber dealers and quiet little housewives, people you'd never expect."

Those who wish to learn more about these arcane ornaments can subscribe to the *Piercing Fans International Quarterly*. Write to: The Gauntlet, 8720 Santa Monica Blvd., Los Angeles, CA 90069. This is a big, full-color glossy that covers all aspects of piercing. There are even letter columns for people seeking "Pin Pals."

TRANSVESTITES

Q: As a struggling actor in a small pond—Portland—I wonder if I couldn't double my possibilities for work if I were able to audition for female parts as well as male roles. *Tootsie* has inspired me. Will I get lynched here in the provinces? What about my baritone voice?

—CY

A: There are always too few acting roles for the talented chromosomal females in this town. If you're just out to prove you're the best woman for the job, go to it. If you're trying to pull an affirmative action scam, you may attract a few bra burners inclined to torch yours while you're wearing it. Competition is hot.

Figure, too, that there will be flak from females who resent the guys disguised as women because they have unforgivably slim hips and because they dedicate themselves to that pink brand of femininity that our mothers wished on us whenever a frog went through the laundry in the pocket of our jeans.

Those males who aren't inclined to bash you may even harbor sympathy for the project. The taxi driver who gave The Slicer a lift to Darcelle XV the other night seemed like an easygoing sort until I asked how he felt about men dressing as women.

"Hey! I can understand it!" he flashed. "When I was a kid I was fascinated by women's clothes, but my mother said I was weird so I shut it down. It would be interesting to see if people treat you differently as a woman than they treat you as a man."

Public reaction aside, disguising gender isn't that simple, and a baritone voice would need special attention. There wasn't time to ask the cabby about the voice problem. A few minutes later the Darcelle spotlight was pounding the red velvet stage curtain in time to a tape of *Thus Spake Zarathustra* to introduce the premier professional female impersonators of Portland. If anybody could get it together to do the job right it ought to be these pros.

Well, the quasi-Rockettes do have great moves, fine legs and hilariously winning ways, but they don't talk. Ninety percent of the show is dance with lip-syncing to tapes of female singers. The chat is all from Darcelle, the Empress, whose voice resembles Janis Joplin gargling ground glass.

The costume gew-gaws and the glitter of stage and lights and music lend a lot of oomph to the flickering Gestalt that entertains; the audience knows it's all illusion. But could Darcelle audition for a soap opera and get away with it? Could Darcelle sidle up to the bar at Cassidy's and order a virgin Mary without the bottle jockey reading "her" like the Sunday funnies?

According to social worker B.J. Seymour, voice is a critical problem for men trying to pass as women. B.J. is a small, fastidious woman. Her stockings and shoes are always color matched, and her diction is always energetic and precise. She talks like a voice coach, which is not surprising. Among her many endeavors, B.J. numbers voice coaching of a very specific kind.

It was after business hours and the southwest Portland clinic was closed when B.J. unlocked the door and invited The Slicer in. The waiting room had thin blinds, electric-orange sofa cushions, and prominent No Smoking signs. That evening the space was to serve as a classroom for B.J. and her students.

The five students drifted in, each carrying a small cassette recorder. They were tall, deep-breasted, well-dressed "ladies" with gallant carriage. Suzie and Jaimie are in their 30s. Linda, Ellen and Ronnie are contemplating retirement. They greeted each other cheerfully, smoothed their tasteful Lane Bryant skirts and crossed elegantly gleaming legs to display graceful ankles and discreetly coquettish high heels. They activated their recorders, and B.J. doled out parts in the play that the class was to read aloud, *The Women*, by Clare Boothe Luce. The redoubtable Luce would have been intrigued by the interpretation of her biting dialogue and by the chuckles that circulated the room during the bitchier passages.

Director B.J. broke in with delivery tips: "More breath, ladies…These soft vowels are a good opportunity to draw out the sound…Soften those R's; we need almost a Southern drawl here…." Seymour avoided raising the pitch of the male voices and relied on each student's available range and changing mannerisms. She skated over hard consonant sounds that could deepen the pitch and emphasized breath in delivery. "We can each develop a wardrobe of voices," she said.

In the more mundane parts of their lives, the five students are successful business or professional people. They are educated, witty and male. Jaimie is homosexual. The others have wives and children who, in most cases, know that their hobby is dressing up in women's clothes.

According to Seymour, "Even transsexuals who have had

radical surgery and intense hormone treatments, and who look totally female, still have male voices and speech mannerisms. Voice is the last and most difficult barrier to adjustment in their female roles." Transsexual clients are referred to Seymour by psychiatrists, and she sees them in private one-to-one sessions. The group classes are only for cross-dressers.

An article by Seymour appeared in the "Forum" page of the *Oregonian* on July 10, 1984, with the headline,"Cross-dressing: Useful and Therapeutic." The article discussed transvestism as a method for men caught in rigidly repressive male roles to express feminine aspects of their personalities. The man who wants to do this, wrote Seymour, "has to either stay in the closet or carry off the masquerade so effectively that he won't be caught.... I'm teaching them to play the roles believably so they can be their whole selves without getting into trouble."

Linda explains that it's not always that easy. "My first wife couldn't handle it at all," she says. "My second wife thinks it's a great lark. She teaches me things: how to dress...how to put on a coat as a woman would."

"I'm gay," says Jaimie, "and you'd expect gays to be more tolerant, but when I came out as Jaimie, Jim lost a lot of friends."

They have all been cross-dressing for years, and they agree that the experience has made them more understanding of women than are most men. The difference in the way they are treated when dressed as females, they say, is dramatic.

The ladies have all seen Dustin Hoffman in the film *Tootsie*. They give him good reviews, except for Ronnie: "Hoffman had so much help—dressers and makeup experts and an expensive prosthetic device to change the shape of his mouth—there wasn't a hint of the work and struggle we go through on our own. It was too easy." Coach B.J. gives Hoffman's voice work good grades. "You'll notice that he adopted a touch of Southern drawl to soften his delivery," she points out.

Linda stresses that Seymour's class is not a therapy group. "We're not interested in analysis or probing heavy encounters," she explains. "We're interested in enjoying what we do, not worrying about it." The ladies are not at all concerned with being "cured." They are intent on learning to be better, more convincing cross-dressers.

"We have supportive socializing groups for cross-dressers and transsexuals all over the country," says Linda. "Here in Portland there's the Northwest Gender Alliance (P.O. Box 13173, Portland, OR 97213). We have regular social gatherings and invite speakers or makeup experts. Every other year on the Oregon Coast there is a weeklong event with people from all over the States and several other countries. A rich Portlander hosts it on his property and we have a marvelous time. Ellen was elected Grande Dame last year."

The Slicer complains that cross-dressers are inevitably better groomed than she is and that they make her feel inadequate as a female. "Oh, but we work hard at what you take for granted," they explain.

They laugh about the beard problem. "What we don't know about beard covers! First you shave *very* close. That's why we're such cheap dates. We can't stay out more than three hours before it starts sprouting through!"

Going out for a drink is a risky adventure. "You have to accept being read," says Ronnie. "People are going to see through you and you just have hope that they'll become accustomed to it."

TATTOOS

Q: Why does the general populace still consider a tattoo the domain of bikers and convicts? Now based in Portland, I am a long-term employee (read "high-up") of a multinational organization. During a three-year stint in Japan, I sought out a "national treasure" in the form of a 65-year-old artisan who labored (sans electrical equipment) on my biceps and shoulder for many hours...resulting in an ornate Japanese design full of cultural meaning and artistic merit. But, at the largely upscale athletic club (you know the initials) where I regularly work out and swim, I am avoided as if I were a past president of the Hell's

Angels who somehow used drug money to force his way through the membership committee. Should I consider starting a support group for upscale males to promote better understanding of this art?

— *Marked for Life, but Enjoying It*

A: Despite the volumes that have been written on the psychopathology of the tattoo, "Marked" is not alone. The streets of Portland are flowing with male and female characters, disguised in preppy, yuppy, or bank-blank duds, who are secretly and permanently ornamented. A nurse acquaintance, suddenly displaying a trailing orchid on her shoulder, says her artist comes down from Seattle periodically and always has a line of waiting clients, many of whom are in the medical profession.

"Long-term commitment always gets the hairy eyeball," says Mary Jane Haake of Dermagraphics, the lush, upscale tattoo studio in downtown Portland. Haake agrees that there is a lot of anti-tattoo prejudice around. "People don't differentiate between self-mutilation—what kids do to themselves or what bored prisoners do to themselves—and a work of art…. It seems like every criminal on TV has a tattoo. An HBO special on the Green River murders actually said at one point, 'You can tell the victims are prostitutes. They all have tattoos….'"

Haake, the first graduate of the Northwestern College of Fine Arts to earn a bachelor's degree in dermagraphics, created quite a furor with her 1981 thesis project. The half-dozen tattooed people she had standing on display at the Portland Art Museum had the administration insisting that they be roped off from the public and that they stand absolutely silent with their faces to the wall. The old story goes that the museum's bricks were originally pale pink but turned red with embarrassment when *P.M. Magazine* filmed those tattoos.

In Japan, tattoos are often associated with the Yakuza, a Mafialike organized crime ring whose trademark is a bodysuit tattoo—although, according to Haake, for the Yakuza, what is "more typical is missing digits on their hands, because the group punishes infractions by cutting off a segment of a finger."

"Of course I'm prejudiced myself," acknowledges Haake. "I'm prejudiced against ugly tattoos."

The National Tattoo Association estimates that one out of ten adults in the United States has some kind of tattoo other than the corrective work that colors scars or repairs lip lines or brows. (The new rage for permanent eyeliner is a flakeoff of the corrective version of tattooing.)

Portland boasts at least three shops in addition to Haake's. Each artist and studio has a particular style. When a client wants a skull or some other classic Americana, Haake sends him or her to the other shops, where such traditions are executed well, despite the 1978 retirement of maestro Bert Grimm, who retired and lived in Seaside until his death in 1985.

Dermagraphics is consistently booked to capacity weeks or even months in advance. Haake works with 60 customers a week and, at $100 per hour, the trade does not consist of drunken sailors. "My average male customer," says Haake, "is either an engineer or a doctor.... The engineers just love the clean graphic lines and the doctors want to set themselves apart from all the sick, naked flesh they see."

Women, however, are Haake's major market. They wouldn't go into a street shop but they can pay a discreet visit to Haake's office building location as though the visit were a dental appointment. "These hard-as-nails business women come in, armored in suits and spike heels," says Haake, "and get a flowing, delicate tattoo to express who they *really* are." In general, such upper-crust tattoos are private expressions not intended for public display, and it's easy to understand the joy of having a secret dragon up one's sleeve.

Those concerned with bequeathing their tattoos along with the rest of their estate should know that it is troublesome but not illegal. The problem lies in finding a friendly mortician willing to remove the skin, and a taxidermist skilled enough to preserve the hide without destroying the color.

Moral and aesthetic support is available from organizations such as the National Tattoo Association (P.O. Box 2063, New Hyde Park, NY 11040), which sends out a magazine every other month and sponsors an international tattoo convention annually.

HEELS

Q: As a fan of females in general, I confess myself delighted by high-heeled shoes. Yet it must be exquisitely painful to teeter along on one's toes, and I sometimes feel guilty for enjoying the sight of an elegant, confident woman in 3-inch spikes. The high-heeled shoe is obviously forced on women to satisfy the aesthetic joy of men at that mysterious magic worked on the female ankle and calf by a suavely designed pump.

— *Guilty Pleasure*

A: Although high spikes are obviously not suited to long jaunts or sprinting, a shoe that fits well is not painful. There are a lot of cultural factors at work when a woman chooses to wear high heels. Sex appeal is just part of it. Conventions of propriety and professionalism vary, but high heels, like long fingernails, are also status labels indicating that the wearer is not required to milk cows, haul water, mine coal or do anything else that requires good traction at the extremities.

The history of high heels goes back thousands of years and suggests two traditional motives: a) keeping the tootsies dry, and b) looking taller.

The butchers of medieval Europe often wore platform clogs to keep their feet out of the blood that flooded the floors of the abattoir. Actors in the ancient Greek theater wore built-up boots or sandals that hoisted them a foot off the floor.

Tallness has always been a big deal in Western culture. Napoleon's complex concerned his height, and males have sought to exploit a vertical illusion as often as females have. While the ladies of the French court were still wearing floor-length dresses over their high heels, the male courtiers were displaying 4-inch heels, skintight socks and knee pants that flaunted the development of their calves.

Our Pilgrim fathers were in modest 2-inch Cuban heels and

plus fours, but they probably twisted their shapely ankles on Plymouth Rock.

A successful local professional woman told The Slicer, "I'm 5-foot-3" and I never appear at the office without 4-inch heels. There's a subtle psychological disadvantage to being short in this culture. The tall people I work with tend to listen just a tad more attentively when I'm disguised as 5-foot-7".

Mychal Thompson does not wear high heels. Prince barely tops 5 feet, and he always wears high heels.

GENDERED FASTENINGS

Q: What reasonable explanation is there for why men's and women's clothing fastens on opposite sides? Is there a historical significance? None of the girls at the office know why there's a difference, and my question has even stumped Dear Abby and Ann Landers. Any ideas?

— *Easy Ed*

A: Abby and Ann must have forgotten to ask the Great Librarian. When gossip, the phone book and the bartender all fail, The Slicer lays questions on the altar at the central branch of the Multnomah County Library. The vestals who guard the sanctum have yet to fail. Anne Goetz in the art and music department discovered the answer in a book called *Accessories of Dress*, by Katherine Morris Lester (published in 1940 by Charles A. Bennett).

Originally, it seems, all clothes buttoned, clasped or hooked right flap over left. That is, the holes were on the right flap of the wearer's shirt and the buttons were on the left flap. Then came the sword. The Licer recalls reader D.T. of Beaverton, who explained that we hop on horses from the beasts' left side because most men, being right-handed, carried their swords on their left sides for fast draws. That way, the right leg is the one that swings up and over. The rider with a sword in scabbard just sticks the left foot in the stirrup and doesn't dump the sword out onto the ground or get jabbed in the back. Well, this button business is similar.

A sword worn on the left side might catch or snag in a shirt or coat flap that buttons right over left. Women's clothing stayed in the old way, but sword-carrying men switched their buttons to the other side to avoid getting hung up. The tradition stays on. There is no connection with left and right brain lobe development, believe me.

BUTTON UPDATE I:

Q: Weeks have passed and no one has written to inform The Slice of the true reason why men's and women's garments button on opposite sides. I guess it's up to me.

When people traveled in horse-drawn carriages, it was customary for men to sit on the right and women on the left. The convention of buttoning shirts and blouses on different sides effectively prevented ladies (or gentlemen) from revealing unseemly expanses of flesh when leaning forward in a carriage. Readers may want to speculate on the decline of morals since the introduction of automobiles with left-hand drive.

— *Auto Enthusiast*

BUTTON UPDATE II: The Feb. 27 Slice explained the

reason why men's and women's clothes button in opposite directions. The wearing of swords on the left hip, we claim, caused men to switch their buttons so as not to get their weapons hung up on the flaps.

Fashion merchandiser Deborah Richert offers another version. Richert says her instructors at Oregon State University taught that when buttons were becoming popular, most women had attendants to help them dress.

"It's easier for someone else to button you if the buttons are on your left and the buttonholes are on your right," says Richert. "Men buttoned themselves, and it's easier for the garment's wearer to button from left to right."

The Slicer finds it difficult to imagine a world in which "most" women had attendants but finds it easy to comprehend a sword-littered culture. We stand by the sword theory.

UPHOLSTERY PROBLEMS

Q: Why are all the women's bathing suits designed for women whose pubic-hair growth pattern corresponds to that of a 13-year-old girl? And my next question is, why do so many women shave, use depilatories, not swim, etc., in compliance with this ridiculous standard? If they sold nothing but C-cup bras would we all go out and get silicon shots so we could wear them?
— *Pubic Hair on My Thighs Like Most Adult Women*

A: The Slicer has no idea whether most adult women have hair on their thighs and is not dying to find out. But not all bathing suits are crotch-cut display items from the *Sports Illustrated* swimsuit issue. Katherine Hansen, merchandise manager for women's swimwear at Jantzen, Inc., says that company produces a number of non-clunky skirted styles that cover the upper thigh and hip. She also suggests asking sales clerks for "boy leg" styles that have a low leg. In general, says Hansen, all manufacturers have been lowering legs in response to customers' tirades on behalf the real human body. Hansen further states that many of the swimsuits in the infamous *S.I.* issue are prototypes designed especially for that issue and may never be mass-produced or sold to the public.

5 Language

RAMA KARMA

Q: I see the Launderama, the Glamourama, the Spaceorama, and Fred's Travelrama. It's "rama" this and "orama" that till the cows come home. What the hell does "rama" mean, Slicer?

— *Puzzlerama*

A: As used in these fabricated words, "rama" is derived from the old Greek word *horama* which meant sight. Maybe "orama" is an Irish view. Or maybe not.

The *Morris Dictionary of Word and Phrase Origins* has an enticing tale of "rama." It seems that words such as panorama and cyclorama have been in use for centuries, but the suffix didn't really take off until the 1939 World's Fair in New York. That was where General Motors installed its hit exhibition of the fantasy future in hot mobiles and called the show "Futurama." The exhibit was such a smash that imitators such as Foodorama and Healthorama sprang up immediately and have never completely died off.

The international Vedantic religious movement is named after Rama Krishna. Rama in this case is the name of the seventh incarnation of the god Vishnu. There is also a tribe native to southeastern Nicaragua named Rama.

The American drug culture, according to Spears' *Slang and*

Euphemism, has used the term "rama" to mean marijuana since the early 1900s.

RABBLE BABBLE

Q: What can you tell me about speaking in tongues? Several celebrity types such as the 700 Club's Pat Robertson and Mrs. Pat Boone claim to have this talent. Is there any recorded case where someone spoke in tongues in the presence of a qualified linguist who would have had the expertise to distinguish ancient Hebrew, for example, from modern gibberish? I believe that miracles do occur, but when members of a certain religious persuasion make rather frequent claims of a certain miracle happening to them, then my suspicion is aroused. What do you have to say about this?

— *Neal*

A: In The Slicer's opinion, speaking in tongues is usually hysterical gobbledygook and is occasionally outright charlatanism.

Speaking in tongues is technically known as glossolalia, from the Greek *glossa*, of or pertaining to the tongue, and *lalein*, to talk or babble. The *American Heritage Dictionary* defines it as "fabricated nonmeaningful speech, especially associated with certain schizophrenic syndromes," and also as "the gift of tongues."

Jeff Mayhew of Northwest Skeptics kindly pitched in to help The Slicer on this one. Between us we discovered only one formal linguistic study. Mayhew writes: "Eugene Nida of the American Bible Society analyzed tongue speech on a tape recording and concluded that it bore no resemblance to any known language, ancient or modern. He was assisted by specialists in more than 150 aboriginal languages spoken in some 25 countries."

This does not disturb the glossolaliacs because most of them don't claim to be speaking ancient Hebrew or any other mortal tongue. It is supposed to be an unknown, divinely inspired language. In many cases the speaker has no notion of what is being said or meant and is thought to be an instrument through which a divine entity is heard. Others interpret the tongue as a language for speaking to God, not to mortals.

Speaking in Tongues is referred to in several entries in the Bible, sometimes as intelligible and inspired, sometimes as inspired but unintelligible. The phenomenon crops up periodically in Western history but came into its own in the United States beginning in the 19th century. Although currently associated with certain "charismatic" Protestant churches, the phenomenon is also known to occur in some Eastern religions and among some psychopaths.

The practice is controversial in some of the Episcopalian, Presbyterian and Baptist churches in which it occurs. Many Christians view the sporadic interruption of services by loud babbling accompanied by twitching, jerking, sweating and eye rolling as uncouth and lacking in elegance.

As Mayhew points out, little scientific attention has been focused on glossolalia, but "the prevailing opinion is that the phenomenon has its origins in the human psyche, not the heavens."

Psychologists usually associate glossolalia with the form of neurosis known as hysteria. It is thought to be a product of intense susceptibility to suggestion, as in "a good subject for hypnosis," or of a conversion syndrome in which inner turmoil is expressed externally or in physical symptoms. Pertinent to the psychology of tongues is that it is considered an honor and a gift and a sign of special religious standing in those constituencies in which it is common.

A different phenomenon is demonstrated in such cases as the multiple-personality rapist, Billy Milligan. One of Milligan's 24 identities was fluent in Hungarian, a language totally unknown to the rest of Milligan.

There are reported cases of childhood or peripheral exposure to a different language being recorded in an individual's memory to surface as fluency during periods of stress or trauma.

We must never underestimate the creative ingenuity of the human mind.

86'D

Q: Please, for God's sake, tell me where the term "86" came from! Why "86"? Why not "85" or "27"?

— *Why*

A: To be 86'd, for the more decorous readers, means to be cut off from service—usually by a bartender—and ejected from an establishment—usually a bar. Lots of folks think they know the source, but no two of them agree. A casual ten-minute Slice poll came up with five different answers.

Scholar Rick Rubin: "I've heard it's from California Statute Number 86, which allows you to throw someone out of a public place."

Carey, behind the bar at the Goose Hollow Inn: "I thought it had something to do with 'deep-six,' meaning to pitch something into the ocean."

Moses, janitor at the Goose: "The federal limitation of 86 proof for whiskey."

Grant, bartender at Delphina's: "Probably the U.S. military code's 'Section 86,' meaning you've run out of something—ammo or Kleenex—and need more. They'd say '86 ammo' for instance."

The Dictionary of American Slang, by Harold Wentworth and Stuart Flexner, says it is a rhyming slang for "nix" (from the old German meaning nothing) and originally meant "we're out of what you asked for." It later came to mean refusing service to someone who is too drunk.

INSINUENDO

Q: My late grandmother was a rather genteel Southern white woman. She always called candle wax "sperm," as in, for example, "It was a delightful dinner but Mr. Emory got sperm all over the dining room table."

Can you enlighten me as to the origins of this interesting locution, either from the point of view of linguistics or depth psychology?

— *Son of the South*

A: This unusual locution no doubt derives from the once common, though expensive, use of spermaceti in making candles and some cosmetics. Two varieties of toothed—as opposed to baleen—whales, known as sperm whales, were named for spermaceti oil, which was found in organic kegs in the front of their huge squared heads. Some theories propose that the oil serves the whale as a lens to focus sounds produced by the whale in echolocation. The spermaceti solidifies in cool air, forming a fine wax.

DRUNKEN SAILORS

Q: Could you please enlighten us as to the etymology of the expression "three sheets to the wind"? We know it denotes a state of inebriation, and we sort of like the image it conjures up, but where the hell did it come from? And why *three* sheets?

— Two Bored Gradual Students

A: This old English sailors' slang varies in the number of sheets, suggesting progressive degrees of drunkenness. "A sheet in the wind" means "half-drunk," according to the Oxford English Dictionary. The O.E.D., incidentally, defines "sheet" in this usage as a rope or a chain attached to the bottom corners of a sail to hold it in place or change directions. Two sheets to the wind would mean one whole sail flapping uselessly. We presume that three sheets in such disarray mean a sail and a half out of control. Authors Richard Dana, Anthony Trollope and Robert Louis Stevenson are all quoted as using some form of this slang in print.

SLIGHTING WORDS

Q: My Italian relatives tell me that the term "wop" comes from the Italian word *guappo*, meaning a big, good-looking man. If so, how did it get such a nasty tone when delivered on the playground?

— Big, Good-Looking Wop

A: The term's derivation from *guappo* is one common theory of the etymology. Wop is generally thought to be the acronym of "without passport" or "without papers." The ugly tone is an example of the old saw, "Words don't mean, people mean."

CROW DU JOUR

Q: The night crew here reads your column weekly. We would like to find out the history of the phrase "to eat crow" or "eating crow." One possibility we raised is that the peons and/or groundskeepers attached to old English estates demonstrated humility by "eating crow," probably the only type of meat they could obtain. What's the truth? We burn with anticipation.

— *Mitch for the Night Crew*

A: The tale goes back to the Anglo-American War of 1812 when—and the versions vary slightly—a man shot a crow and another man forced him to take a raw bite of it.

Brewer's Dictionary of Phrase and Fable tells how a New Englander on a hunting trip during a temporary armistice, unwittingly crossed the British lines. For lack of better game, the American shot a crow. A British officer heard the shot, caught him, took his gun and, by way of humiliation, forced him at gunpoint to take a bite of the bird. Having munched, the New Englander disarmed the officer and held the gun on him, forcing him to eat the rest of the crow. The story became public when the officer reported the violation of the armistice.

Picturesque Expressions, edited by Urdang, Hunsinger and La Roche, claims that an American soldier in the same war shot a pet crow and the bird's owner forced him at gunpoint to eat the brute. Recapturing his rifle, the soldier then forced the crow's owner to finish off the carcass.

INSULT ETYMOLOGY

Q: Where does the term "cracker" come from? I've always heard it used to refer to bigoted, uneducated white trash.

— *Keeping My Slurs Straight*

A: Originally, "cracker" was applied to the poor farming population of the Southeastern United States whose dietary staple was cracked corn.

GUEST GHOSTS
Q: Why do we "toast" someone with a drink? Isn't that an odd term for such a salute?

— *In My Cups*

A: The custom started in the sixth century B.C. in Greece, where poisoning had become a common path around divorce, as well as a method of eliminating enemies. It was a friendly thing for a host to sip first from the decanter, as proof that the wine was not toxically spiked, and for his guests to follow suit in an expression of faith in his hospitality. We have this from Charles Panati, and his excellent volume, *Extraordinary Origins of Everyday Things*, Harper & Row, 1987. Panati goes on to explain that the Romans adopted the custom and tossed a bit of burnt or toasted bread into their wine because charcoal reduces the acidity of liquids and the table wine of the day was less than mellow.

The Slicer has a hunch that dedicating a snort to persons present or not, ideas, nations, projects and the like, may hark all the way back to the religious custom of pouring libations as sacrifices to gods or souls or whatnot.

PINNING DOWN THE BUCK
Q: What is this famous "buck" that gets passed around—you know, the one that stops at the president's desk? Is that American currency? If so, it's the only buck I've ever heard of that didn't tend to stick to any fingers it touched.

— *Buck-Passer*

A: "Passing the buck" is a phrase from the frontier days of poker playing. According to *The Story of English* by McCrum,

Cran and MacNeil, "The buck was the buckhorn-handled knife placed in front of the dealer and passed by a player who did not care to deal the next hand."

The next question is, what was that knife for? So the dealer could defend himself if accused of cheating? Or as a threat that it would be used on the dealer if he were caught cheating?

The game of poker, claim the same authors, derives from a three-card French game called *poque* that was enormously popular in the Wild West.

"Buck" as in moola, greenbacks, bread, grease, smagollahs, scratch or dollars, comes from "buckskins." Deerhides were a form of currency for the trappers and hunters who gathered and sold them even after beaver skins were no longer the rage in the *haut monde*.

BOSS WORD

Q: My boss always calls himself the "honcho" of our organization. Out of curiosity I looked it up in several Spanish dictionaries but couldn't find it. Does the word "honcho" have some obscene slang meaning? If so, I want to know the next time the boss starts "honcho-ing" around.

— *Honcho'ed Out*

A: Wrong language. According to McCrum, Cran and MacNeil, in *The Story of English*, honcho derives from the Japanese word meaning squad leader. Its use in this country dates from the American occupation of Japan. Originally a noun, as used by this reader's boss, honcho took on a popular verb function in the mouth of John Erlichman during the Senate Watergate hearings.

NIGHTMARE BLAST

Q: "Petard," Slice. What is it? As in "Hoist by his own..." Since I was a small boy I've had hideous nightmares about being snatched up by a block and tackle clamped onto my most private organ and being dragged into the air, screaming, until the thing, my thing, rips off and I fall…and fall…and jerk awake in a sick sweat. The error of reading *Hamlet* to a toddler. So, petard—as in saltpeter, which is thought to be administered in prison food to stunt one's sexual appetites? Help!

— *Petard Paranoid*

A: Sheesh! According to a ratty but functional old *Webster's Third New International Dictionary* that happened to be lying around on the table in the Multnomah County Library, the word petard comes from the French word meaning "to break wind" or "the expulsion of intestinal gas." Petard is defined as a metal or wood case containing explosives for use in breaking down a door or gate or breaching a wall during a siege. We're talking old-timy stuff here, naturally. What Hamlet says is, "For /'tis the sport to have the engineer/Hoist with his own petar; and /'t shall go hard/But I will delve one yard below their mines/And blow them at the moon."

As for saltpeter, that is potassium nitrate, an ingredient in black powder that might have been part of the recipe for a petard, but the etymology is different. (For a discussion of saltpeter and sex, see Chapter 1, "Limp Sticks"…The Slice.)

Q: What joke has the punch line: "You don't know shit from Shinola"?

— *Curious in Milwaukie*

A: Various folks, over the past few decades, have felt called upon to use this phrase in conversation with The Slicer. Few of them, unfortunately, were joking. It seems clear that this is not a mere punch line, but is itself the whole shebang. It belongs to a particular class of insult intended to demonstrate the depth of ignorance—either on a specific subject or in general—suffered by the subject, "you." Other examples of parallel structure in the *insultus ignoramus* class are: "You don't know your ass from your elbow," "You don't know your ass from a hole in the ground," and so on. Few of these alternates have quite the euphonious alliteration of "shit from Shinola." Few achieve the graphic accuracy of this comparison. (Those who are unfamiliar with Shinola—a thick, waxy shoe polish that commonly occurs in shades of black, brown and cordovan—will never appreciate the depth of perception brought to play in this image.) The phrase is, in The Slicer's opinion, a stroke of colloquial genius. While it has inspired many jokes, it is definitely the source rather than the product. The original author of this miniature masterpiece is unknown to The Slicer and may be that prolific character, Anonymous. One suspects, naturally, some innovative drill instructor of either world war's vintage. Military origins would explain the nationwide distribution of the phrase.

Scholars will note that there are many non-parallel subspecies of *insultus ignoramus*, notably the "You wouldn't know a — if it —ed you" and the "What you know about — would fit in a — with room to spare" variations.

6 Natural Curiosity

WHERE TO POST BOTTLE MESSAGES

Q: Do you still answer whimsical questions? In search of romance and adventure, I've decided to start using my empty wine bottles to send messages over the seas to foreign lands. What part of the tide would be best for casting them afloat? Is one part of the coast better than another?

— *Get My Drift*

A: The answer is as whimsical as the question. The Coast Guard, the National Weather Service, the National Oceanic and Atmospheric Administration, Oregon State University's School of Oceanography and the Marine Science Center all took a crack at this seemingly simple question and came up with admissions of puzzlement and relatively little real info.

Dr. Adriana Huyer of OSU says the best season of the year to throw bottles out is the spring, particularly April and May. That's the time when the bottle will have a chance to go out the farthest before it is met by an incoming storm that will push it back toward shore.

All sources agree that the bottle should be thrown early in an outgoing tide. Huyer suggests that the farther north on the coast you are, the better the chance that the bottle will be caught by a prevailing current.

The problem is that the tides and the tidal currents just offshore vary enormously and may reverse themselves from week to week or even overnight.

The odds are enormous that anything you throw into the water at Seaside will drift ashore at Cannon Beach. Of course, you should throw bottles from an open coast, not an estuary. The Coast Guard asks that you please don't throw them into the Columbia because, if there are too many, the odds go up that John Q. Citizen will meet them while cresting the bar in his 17-foot putt-about and not make it home to supper. Besides, there's a good chance that the bottle would just get caught and recirculate forever in the Columbia system.

If you really want that bottle to get to China or Seoul, take a boat out 30 miles or so. Use a thermometer to test the temperature of the water. When you find a spot where the temperature changes radically, throw in the bottle. Huyer says such a spot "at least might be the edge of a major current."

For all our centuries of swooping around on the surface, the ocean is still a mighty mysterious place.

NO BULL

Q: This hunting season the same old question popped up. Why do hunters insist on wearing red or bright orange shirt, coats, hats, and so forth, when they are going to be on foot in cattle-grazing areas? Wouldn't sky blue or yellow be warning enough to keep them from shooting each other without exposing them to getting trampled or gored by a bull?

—*Red on the Range*

A: Bulls are colorblind. The brightness of a color and how much light bounces off it may catch their eyes. Movement is another alarm they respond to. The color itself is irrelevant. On the other hand, most bipedal folks packing projectile weapons in these parts do recognize red or bright orange as a warning or danger signal.

LAWN GONE

Q: As spring approaches I am plunging into despair. The glorious new house that we moved into two years ago is surrounded by an acre of grass. The neighbors insist that we keep the lawn nipped down to velvet levels. The time required—not to mention the caloric output—is outrageous. I don't want to live in an apartment. I can occasionally pay a youngster to do the deed, but all in all, I'm fed up with green.

Where, in heaven's name, did the idea of keeping naturally tall grass cut so short come from?

— *Cut to the Quick*

A: Lawns and ornamental grass plots were left to grow to their natural height for many centuries. According to Charles Panati, in his book, *Extraordinary Origins of Everyday Things*, we can blame golfers and lawn bowlers for the frenzy for mowed lawns. Panati claims that the early 1800s, with the growing passion for golf and lawn bowling in England, were the source of mowed lawns. Be thankful you don't have to cut it in the old, original way: with a scythe.

MERRY GRASS MASS

Q: On the subject of lawns—estate lawns were once kept

mowed short by sheep (as were golf courses, which were originally not much more than pasture). So today the average suburbanite is saying, "I have pasture" (I have animals = true wealth). I think this is the reason men in particular enjoy having a good lawn—they feel an echo of the patriarchal warriors who drove into Europe with herds and Indo-European languages.

And I can't stop here—it's nice to remember that lawn grass is our largest crop. If we devoted that land, fuel, water and fertilizer to grain production we could produce enough to feed Africa and India (I know, transport, yayaya, etc.).

I prefer to have a small lawn (no bigger than a croquet course) and maintain the rest of my domain at a later stage in biological succession—i.e., meadow, shrubs, or trees or bamboo grove. If help is needed, look for someone practicing permaculture, edible landscaping or native-plant landscaping—or preferably all of the above.

— *R. From Bamboo Town*

A: Many of our readers will no doubt benefit from this sage advice. The Slicer has vowed never to have a lawn until she can also afford to hire someone to tend it. The mere words "peat moss" make her nose bleed.

Further, the word is that we *already* grow enough excess, subsidized grain to feed Africa and India, but the federal government buys it and stores it in cavernous warehouses in the Midwest along with mountains of slowly rotting milk products and other foodstuffs.

THE SLIVER VS. THE GREEN FLASH

Q: About a hundred years ago, when I was in college, I saw something I'm not sure I really saw. It was such a cool thing that I've gone to great lengths to see it again and, though I think I've seen it, I'm still not positive. It's called a greenflash, at least that is what I call it. It is supposed to happen when the sun is setting into the horizon of the ocean. You say all the "going, going, goings," and just about the time you say "gone," that last little fingernail clipping of the sun slips behind the water and flashes a split second of green. It's an amazing sight to see, though I might feel better about my sanity if you could confirm it.

—*Flashes of Sanity*

A: I was tempted to dismiss this as hallucinosis, but I knew I couldn't face The Slicer without having explored all the rational explanations of the strange sight. I was informed by the National Weather Service that the so-called "greenflash" is, in fact, a documented phenomenon with a rational, albeit complex, explanation. A January 1960 article in *Scientific American* by D.J.K. O'Connell lists the causes of the greenflash as "dispersion, scattering, and absorption of sunlight by the earth's atmosphere." Don Hipperson of the National Weather Service explains that these conditions make the green color "instantaneously predominant" in the sky. The flash can last anywhere from a fraction of a second to 20 seconds, and may also be seen as blue, violet or even a combination of these colors. The flash involves dispersion of light and is therefore visible only when the air is thickest, and sunlight travels at its longest angle through the atmosphere, i.e. at sunset and sunrise. A clear, hazeless sky is one of the many necessary conditions for the flash, so your best bets for greenflash viewing are in the desert, in mountains or over water.

The greenflash has been a source of controversy for many years and was initially attributed to "retinal fatigue" brought on by overexposure to the bright light of the sun. Flash viewings at sunrise, before anyone's retinas had a chance to become fatigued, dispelled this theory. The search for an explanation for the phenomenon even inspired Jules Verne's 1882 novel, *Le Rayon Vert* (and the subsequent 1986 movie called *Summer*). Those who have been questioning their sanity, or that of their spouses "Honey, I swear, it was bright green" can rest assured that there is a scientific explanation for the greenflash, even if scientists are the only ones who can understand it.

7 Science, Static, Fans & Other Joys of the 20th Century

VOLUME CONTROL

Q: Tell me I'm not going blinky! When watching the all-knowing eye, does it seem to you that the commercials are broadcast at a greater volume than the programs? What gives?
— *Semi-Deaf*

A: Folks have been noticing this phenomenon for years and The Slicer was delighted to have an excuse to ask about it. The broadcast engineers at KATU and KGW in Portland agreed that the commercials are not, repeat *not*, broadcast any louder than the programs. There are even sophisticated computer-operated loudness-control devices to clamp down any accidental beeps above the maximum decibel level. The trick, say these wizards, is that the techniques used to design and produce commercials boost and compress the sound in ways calculated to get viewer attention. Though at no time does the actual volume of a commercial exceed the loudest volume of a regular program, commercials are often designed and produced to be constantly noisy—loud music jingles, fast-talking announcers—instead of having the lulls and split-second silences that occur in a more conversational program. It's really noticeable if the program or movie you're watching doesn't have a constant music sound track. Then the commercial interruptions will blow you out of the room. KGW's master-control operator, Tony Monteverdi, calls this effect "psychological loudness."

The TV stations are acutely aware of this effect and try to avoid irritating their audience with it. Dee Sloan, the irrepressible receptionist at KGW, says as long as she's worked at the station she's been told, "If anyone phones with a complaint about the commercials being too loud, the engineers want to know right away."

DRY CLEANING
Q: What is the dry cleaning process, anyway?
          — *Sheldon Baker, Formerly Wet and Bored in PDX*

A: Dry is a misnomer. Your clothes do get wet, but not with water. Ben Bleich, owner of Bee Tailors and Cleaners on Southwest Salmon Street, spent about an hour trying to explain this process to the washboard consciousness of The Slicer.

This is the story. After your clothes are tagged and then disappear mysteriously, they are sorted into various fabric classifications. Silks are sorted by color. Woolens are separated into light and heavy piles. At that point they *should* be given "prespot" treatment. Mr Bleich's tone suggested that some unnamed inferior cleaners *don't* prespot. The process involves identifying the ingredients of whatever you've dribbled down your front, sat in or rubbed elbows with and attacking the stain with the appropriate noxious chemical. The clothes then are deposited in gargantuan machines with the same wash-rinse-spin cycles as a washing machine. Instead of water the clothes are immersed and agitated in one of several possible solvents. The Slicer's 1953 *American People's Encyclopedia*—24 volumes for 6 bucks at a used book sale—calls these solvents chlorinated hydrocarbons, which is a polite term for petrochemicals. The most commonly used solvent for the machines is perchlorethylene, which Bleich describes as "the most aggressive" of the solvents. Dry cleaners are monitored and restricted as to how many molecules per thousand of these solvents can be released into the atmosphere. As Bleich points out, the more solvent that can be retrieved, filtered and used again, the more money the establishment saves. The spin cycle extracts most of the solvent. In older machines the clothes are then taken out and transferred to a tumble dryer, which extracts more solvent. Newer machines, called dry-to-dry units, do the whole number and produce clean, dry clothes. The clothes then go back to the hand spotter for any stubborn devil stains that need another attack. Then it's on to the finishers who do the pressing, folding or whatever else is involved in the classy "dry cleaner" look. Incidentally, there's no real difference between Martinizing and dry cleaning. Or only as much difference as there is between a hamburger and a McDonald's burger. Martinizing is a franchise process.

WHERE THE PREZ GOES WHEN THE LIGHTS GO OUT

Q: In the event of nuclear war, where would the president and the chiefs of staff go? What kind of shelter would they use? How could they control the war throughout the chaos?

— *Bandit*

A: The Pentagon does not discuss these things with The Slicer, but the odds are that the muckamucks won't be in any of their top-secret holes in the classified ground. They'll be flying miles above the fire and ash storms in one of the most expensive aircraft ever constructed, the Boeing E-4B. This special unarmed plane, known as the advance airborne command post, has masses of navigational and communications equipment, all classified. Speculation says it can talk to high- and low-frequency satellites, displace radio and TV signals and interpret the song of the frying squid. The range is classified, but three days in the air is rumored. The U.S. Air Force currently deploys three of these babies, but neither you nor I are likely to be invited aboard.

FEAR OF FLYING

Q: I am terrified of flying, but love to travel. I recently discovered that a glass of sherry before boarding and another en route makes the process almost tolerable. I've heard many times that flying is the safest way to travel but have never seen any studies. If you could print the statistics it might help soothe my next trip.

— *Bound for Glory*

A: Call up an airline if you want to hear their propaganda. No sane and sapient person really needs to go anywhere that can't be reached by boat. Ever notice that when the Pope climbs out of an airplane, the first thing he does is fall down and kiss the earth? The guy knows something.

SMOKING BENNIES

Q: What are the benefits of smoking?

— *LeB*

A: The *New York Times'* 1985 Christmas gift to its tobacco-smoking readers was a Dec. 25 article which, along with the usual dire (and doubtless true) warnings, discussed some of the lures of nicotine addiction. "Nicotine literally alters the availability of important brain chemicals involved in feelings of reward and well-being," says the *Times*. "There is evidence that cigarettes make task performance easier, improve long-term memory, reduce anxiety, increase tolerance of pain and reduce hunger.... Furthermore, the way smoke is inhaled affects the response. Studies are showing that short, quick puffs—low doses—tend to stimulate or arouse brain function and behavior. Deep, full drags—high doses—create the more sedative, relaxing effects of smoking." So far, researchers have no more idea of how all this happens than they do of how aspirin deadens pain.

The effect of tobacco smoke on non-smoking bystanders is, of course, being used as the pretext for organized, state-supported (in non-tobacco-growing states) discrimination against brown-lunged citizens. The Sonia Corporation is reportedly working on a device that may prevent, or at least delay, the smokers' concentration camp movement. The device, a miniature inhaler, draws in smoke and filters it out of the air within 20 cubic feet of the smoker who wears the machine. The prototype is designed to clip onto the brim of a hat, but earring and tie-clasp models are on the drawing board.

The Iroquois' Revenge, as tobacco is known, does benefit the nation's economy by employing thousands of individuals in growing, packaging and marketing the weed. Consider, too, the number of medical personnel, drug abuse conselors and morticians whose livelihood depends on the aftermath. As a Bugler roller of long standing, The Slicer is convinced that the federal government—despite tsk-tsks from the surgeon general—encourages the tobacco industry because it cuts down on the number and duration of beneficiaries for Social Security.

WHERE THE YELLOW WENT
Q: Why do many toothpaste tubes sport an expiration date? Can toothpaste go bad? Professor Feeblewitz claims that toothpaste has radioactive ingredients to make your teeth whiter, and the expiration date marks their half-life. We don't believe him. Please settle this matter.

— *Elmer*

A: Some toothpastes are drugs, according to Sue Hutchcroft, the consumer affairs officer of the United States Food and Drug Administration office in Seattle. If the stuff contains fluoride or other substances meant to "treat, prevent, cure or ameliorate a disease or bodily condition" (the FDA definition of a drug), the manufacturer is required to print an expiration date. Radioisotopes would probably fall under one of those categories—as in preventing or curing the condition of being alive—if there were any in the tube. Any toothpaste without such a date is regarded, by the FDA at least, as a cosmetic.

FAN DANCE

Q: I have spent another fitful night because of the heat and write to you knowing you can give me the answer to this burning question. In order to cool off my house efficiently, is it better to put the fan in the window and suck the cool outside air in or is it better to blow the hot air out?

— *Fussy from the Heat*

A: Typically, cooling is more efficient if you blow hot air out, according to engineer Al Radys of TRI-M, Inc., the air-conditioning and heating-system outfit. Radys says blowing the air out of your house will create a negative pressure inside that will draw the outside air in.

ICING UP

Q: I've had a question I've wondered about for a long time. How do they turn a hockey rink into a basketball court and vice versa? It seems like a lot of work to rip all the boards up, then pour water down and freeze it! And how do they get those blue and red lines in the ice?

— *Gotta Know*

A: The cement floor is riddled with freezer tubes of ethylene glycol (similar to antifreeze), according to Carl Ahrens, the events manager for Portland's Exposition-Recreation Commission. To make the rink, the floor is cooled to zero degrees and an eighth of an inch of water is sprayed on and freezes. The ice is painted white with fine talcum powder, the lines are painted on with tempera paint, which freezes, and then another half inch of water is sprayed on to freeze. The whole process takes about 12 hours.

Removing the ice means heating the tubes until the floor hits about 68 degrees and the sheet of ice pops loose. A tractor with a blade breaks up the sheet and shoves the shards into a pit. The heated tubes dry the floor rapidly and the basketball boards are laid on top.

If hockey and B-ball are running alternate nights and it's too troublesome to remake ice each time, a subfloor of 2-by-4s and plywood is laid over the ice and the basketball court laid on top. Either process takes about two hours.

8 Population Control Devices: Cars and Streets

CAR BRAS

Q: Why do cars wear bras?

— Pedestrian

A: A local real estate association pays the owner of a 1983 lemon-toned Porsche to park the car in front of my building in an effort to upgrade property values hereabouts. This automobile does, indeed, have an imposing Naugahyde bikini top snugged over its forward protuberances. The garment obviously functions much the same as the see-through plastic slipcovers which my Aunt Myrtle keeps on her nubby turquoise-with-silver-thread, three-piece sectional with matching chairs and ottoman. Myrtle says, "It saves the upholstery for good." I assume "for good" means permanently rather than for glorious social occasions, because the the plastic slipcovers stayed stickily in place for Cousin Thelma's wedding reception and for Uncle Norval's wake.

The car bra, however, is known officially as a stone guard. Scholar and historian Richard Livesey, parts manager for Continental Porsche and Audi, says it is to protect the paint job from being chipped by flying gravel. Although dealers don't usually make an issue of it, Livesey says almost any car with a down-sloping hood could benefit by wearing one.

Cars wear bras in wedding and funeral processions and even while decanting tuxes and taffeta at the Schnitz. Darcelle's car would, of course, wear a padded bra. Obviously all down-sloping prows should be made out of Naugahyde to begin with.

RAISING HOODS—BY MA BARKER

Q: Why do car dealers leave the hoods of the cars on their lots propped open?

— Just Wondering

A: When the hoods are up, the dealer is open for business. The friendly local car salesman says it's to attract attention during daylight hours when flashy lights and neon signs lack pizzazz. Dealers also try to keep someone (an apprentice salesman if the weather's bad) moving around the lot by way of letting the public know the place is ready to deal. The obvious purpose of demonstrating that there actually is an engine in the vehicle is accompanied by practical effects. A hood that is propped open won't get bent hinges, broken locks or scratched paint from being banged open and shut by inexperienced customers 50 times a day.

ON APPROACHING A HOLE IN A HILL

Q: Why the signs that say "tunnel" just before you go through a tunnel? I mean, what difference do they make? Are motorists going to turn around or what? Do they prevent panic? ("My God, Helen, it's dark all of a sudden. Do you think the mountain blew?") Please muckrake your way to the bottom of this. I think it's a scam.

— *A Citizen Against Superfluous Signage*

A: Yes, exactly, to all of the above. Tunnel signs are an acknowledgment of human inclinations to freak out at any change. The philosophy is akin to the rationale behind the saucer under a coffee cup. The saucer-cup attitude is culturally defined. The old-fashioned cup-and-saucer combo admits that people spill and prevents the mess from affecting the upholstery. The current fashion for mugs eschews saucers on the theory that it's natural to spill and leave wet rings on tables—what's natural is good, and plastic doesn't stain anyway. Oriental teacups seem unforgivably smug. No saucer ("We're too cool to spill") and they even abandon the handle ("Only the unenlightened burn their fingers").

Oh, yeah, tunnels. The sign just alerts you to expect a change. Many tunnels are not well lit. Often the road surface is different. On wet or icy days outside, hitting the dry tunnel area changes handling requirements. Consider those signs like DEER CROSSING and FALLING ROCKS that deal with slight probabilities. What percentage of a 24-hour period do you suppose deer spend hiking across a road? At least if a sign says TUNNEL the odds are good that there really is—at the very instant you drive past the sign—a tunnel on the other side. Besides, why begrudge honorable employment to sign painters?

KITTY KILLER FOILED

Q: This is serious. I am in the advanced stages of a major plan for kitty genocide (felinocide). I wash my car. It looks pretty. I leave it out overnight (no garage). There are little footprints all over it in the morning. Millions. I join a SWAT team. I am very angry. Very. Nothing stops them. It is a plot—Communist? Republican? Catholic?—I'm positive. Anyway, I'm arming; a little extreme, yes, I know—but I can't take it anymore. I want a clean pawless auto to drive around. That's not too much to ask of this life, is it? You're my last hope—our last hope (there are thousands of similar preyed-on folk secretly organizing on dark nights). There must be a realistic solution short of mass murder. Most grateful,

—*Corvallis Cat Haters*

A: Look, you can tease the KGB. You can screw the CIA. You can mess with the FBI. You can fiddle with the IRS. But never—listen to The Slicer now, honey—never cause even the mildest form of irritation to the ASPCA. Those people are bad.

The obvious way to protect a car from cat prints is with a car cover. You can put a thick blanket or tarp over the car and tie it down so it won't slip. You can get a thin nylon cover for 40 bucks or so. You can get a medium-priced canvas-top/flannel-inside cover. Or you can go bananas and order one of the three-layer, bonded, water-repellent, breathable Technalon items from Cover-Craft that is custom fit to your buzzmobile for $150 or so.

SIREN SONGS

Q: Why do some emergency vehicle sirens sometimes make long, drawn-out calls (wwwuuuuuuhhhh-OOOOOOOOOO-uuuuuuuhhhh) and other times short bursts (wow-wow-wow-wow)? Why do we hear combinations of the two siren songs? Do they have different meanings? Does the siren mechanism automatically change its tune or does the driver do it? And why am I writing this letter instead of doing my job?

—*Serenaded by Sirens*

A: The driver controls the siren, and the various sounds have no particular code meaning. In general, the wail is used in free-moving traffic and the short barks are used at intersections to get the public's attention. Firetrucks use their deep-throated air horns along with their sirens at intersections. Portland Police Sgt. Scott Anderson, in charge of emergency-dispatcher training at Kelly Butte, explains that the changes of pitch in the shorter bursts are thought to be easier for people to locate in direction and distance. "Downtown, for example, where there are a lot of tall buildings, the sound will bounce around a lot and it can be difficult to tell how close it is or what direction it's coming from. We think the changes in pitch alleviate that somewhat." Kevin Anderson, ambulance dispatcher for Care Ambulance, agrees and points out that different years and makes of vehicle have different siren voices.

WORN OUT

Q: What happens to all the rubber that gets worn off tires?

—Tire Biter

A: The amount of rubber whittled off by the friction between tire and pavement, about a third of an inch of tire every 40,000 miles, may at first seem an insignificant amount of black dust. But when one considers that in 1986 some 2,624,758 motorized vehicles were registered in Oregon, each capable of excreting as much as a half pound of rubber a year, it's clear that this dust actually represents a mountain of petroleum compound.

If it could somehow be gathered and recycled, this otherwise useless waste matter might serve to prevent an entire population of unwanted pregnancies, not to mention countless sexually transmitted diseases.

Where does all this rubber actually go? In my first investigative task as slave to The Slicer, I contacted Spencer Erickson, the air-quality expert of the Department of Environmental Quality. According to Erikson, after these particles become airborne, one of two things might happen to them. In their tireless search for a second home, the newly formed pieces of rubber are either ground into the road or deposited in street gutters and eventually washed into the nearest river or sewage treatment plant.

As I coughed on the nearby smoke of one of The Slicer's hand-rolled cigarettes, I couldn't help but wonder if such tire particles might also be causing harm to our respiratory systems.

Erickson assured me I could breathe a petroleum-free sigh of relief. Erickson says a particle must be smaller than 10 microns (a micron is .001 millimeters) to affect the human respiratory system by EPA standards. Larger particles are removed in the upper regions of the tract, such as the nose, by means of phlegm, before they reach the lungs. Because of the mechanical nature of the process by which rubber is removed from a tire, Erickson claims the particles produced are generally 10 times the size of harmful fragments.

AUTO IMPORTS

Q: The automobile is an American invention. True or false?

— *Stumped at a Greasemonkey's Kegger*

A: False. *The Dictionary of Misinformation*, by former Portland State University professor Tom Burnam, punctures this myth along with several hundred others in common use. Both the invention and the first production of an automobile are credited to Germany. Karl Benz patented the Benz Patent Motor Wagon in Mannheim in 1885, the same year that Gottlieb Daimler patented his own, independently developed creation, the Daimler, in Stuttgart. The Duryea clan introduced the first automobile in America in 1894, according to Burnam.

HEIRS TO THE HITCHING POST

Q: My boyfriend doesn't believe me when I tell him that the metal rings bolted to the sidewalks and curbs in various parts of town were for tying up horses. Isn't it so?

— A.J.

A: Yes. They're called "horse rings" and served the same purpose as did the private lawn-jockey statues of hideous yore.

TIMING IS THE THING

Q: Do all traffic lights have the same second allotment to yellow lights? If so, how was this universal arrived at? If not, how are different intervals decided upon? What is the mathematical equation?

— Slow to Stop

A: City Traffic Engineer Bill Kloos says the basic minimum time for a yellow light to last is three seconds. The yellow is set to last longer when approach speeds at an intersection are higher. The higher-speed arterials have much longer yellow lights. There is also one full second interval of all red before the one-way green flashes on.

Readers frequently write in with questions about traffic lights. "Seeking Houdini" is convinced that a certain intersection on Southeast Belmont Street is the current residence of the spirit of his hero, Harry. This reader claims that on Halloween each year, the light blinks out Morse code for "Help. Trapped in circuit board. H.H." The Slicer has tried to inform "Seeking" that Houdini died before circuit boards were in use and that it must be somebody else—perhaps Howard Hughes—but to no avail.

Another reader, "Upwardly Mobile," writes that aliens are trying to communicate with her through the yellow blinking signal at her corner. "Upwardly" reports that she is more than willing to make contact, travel to far galaxies and submit to any tests required in the name of interplanetary peace. She simply needs the answering code.

Various readers feel that the government or their insurance broker is spying on them via traffic lights or that malicious plots to disrupt their passage through traffic are perpetrated by the genie of one light or another.

9 Grub

ESPRESSO DEFINED

Q: What exactly is "espresso"? Is it just expensive coffee ground on the spot? All coffee is imported (isn't it?), so why the 50 cents to $1 price difference? Is "espresso" more nutritious? Does it taste better? Is it alcoholic?

As a recent immigrant to the City of Roses from rural east Marion County, I have been wondering about this since arriving in the metropolis. Now that I'm a city slicker, I suppose I should know.

— *E. Arthur*

A: Espresso is Italian for "quick" and it refers to a particular way of brewing coffee. Various espresso machines have been devised, but the basic idea always is to heat water under pressure above the boiling point and then force it rapidly through the ground coffee. The hotter the water, the more flavor is extracted from the coffee. The shorter the brewing time, the less bitter the coffee.

Espresso also is used to designate the grind and the specific dark-roasted varieties of coffee which are thought to produce the best flavor by this method. Jim Roberts at Coffee People says good espresso coffees all come from South or Central America because the beans grown there can be dark-roasted without crumbling from the heat.

The rationale for the expense of espresso probably should include that each cup has to be made separately, that the coffee itself costs more, that the machines cost plenty and that espresso freaks are consistently willing to pay that much for it. It is not alcoholic. It is an acquired taste, not unlike a fondness for 1,000-year-old eggs.

DECAF

Q: As a concerned coffee drinker I have often wondered what sort of diabolical process coffee beans are subjected to in order to "decaf."

In line with this question, is there also a process that neuters tea?

— Idly Nervous About De-Caf

Q: My decaffeinated friend and I would like to know how they get the caffeine out of coffee. We understand there are at least two methods: solvent extraction and water extraction. We are especially interested in how the caffeine is extracted from whole beans and whether or not there is any risk of solvent residue in the former method.

— Sincerely, No-Caf

A: The Slicer drinks instant caffeine-full coffee by the bucket at home. When I want real coffee it means high-octane, megavoltage espresso suitably doctored with cream and sugar. It also means that somebody else prepared it. This is simply to explain the ignorance on this topic that drove me up to the Coffee People store on Northwest 23rd Avenue. The original Coffee Man, Jim Roberts, patiently explained the processes. It seems the act of decaf always is performed on green, whole beans, which then are roasted and ground or left whole.

The solvent extraction process can be done in two ways. The direct-contact method has the beans soaked in a tank of solvent solution. The solvent, methylene chloride, is a familiar byproduct of automobile exhaust. The clever chemical bonds with caffeine. Methylene chloride also has the advantage of an extremely low boiling point, around 90 degrees Fahrenheit. It evaporates very easily, taking the caffeine with it, as the beans are heated and then roasted. This is the method generally used for canned coffees. Gourmet coffee, as Roberts calls it, generally is decaffed by the indirect method. In this gourmet process, the green beans are suspended above boiling water and steam is forced through them. As the coffee heats, the cells and pores open, allowing the steam to displace the oil from the coffee. All of the caffeine as well as the flavor components are in that oil. The oil goes into a tank of that same solution, methylene chloride, where the caffeine bonds with the solvent. A small portion of the flavor components in the oil also will bond to the solvent, but if the solvent is used repeatedly it will cease leeching flavor but continue to leech caffeine out of the oil. When the oil-solvent mix is boiled, the solvent and its guest caffeine boil away through a distillery coil or something, and all that's left is the flavorful oil. The beans are then soaked in the oil, reabsorb it, are roasted and are sent off for sale.

The coffee industry folks are not paranoid about this process, explains Roberts, because they send samples of the decaffed beans out to be tested periodically by independent laboratories. In tests looking for parts-per-million, there is no detectable trace of the volatile substance remaining after the drying and roasting process. Presumably, brewing coffee with boiling water would further prevent the frisky stuff from hanging around.

The water process—a patented method employed by only one company in Germany—uses only water, no chemicals. It does, however, soak out many of the flavor elements along with the caffeine. Roberts says it costs about $1 more a pound than the other gourmet items and has a relatively limited selection.

His store carries only seven varieties of water-decaffed coffee.

A third method is to follow the indirect solvent process but use the recently introduced ethyl acetate as the solvent. This stuff is an all-natural item derived from fruit.

Tea can be and is decaffeinated. A detectable solvent residue in some tea caused the Food and Drug Administration to ban the sale of decaf tea last year but it has reappeared on the market recently with a different process behind it.

So there you go. After all that, The Slicer needs a cup of coffee.

DECAF DECEPTIONS: Certain coffee and tea products are being advertised locally as "naturally 97 percent caffeine-free." The line is meant to appeal to those decaffeinated folk who are suspicious of the chemical process used to remove the drug from coffee beans. The statement actually is misleading and does not indicate a low-caffeine product.

Please note that most canned coffees consist of robusta-type coffee grown at low elevations, blended with some Arabica varieties from higher elevations. These standard supermarket canned coffees contain 3 percent caffeine by weight and also truthfully can be called "naturally 97 percent caffeine-free." Most teas also contain 3 percent caffeine by weight. The so-called gourmet coffees are almost all from the Arabica species and are grown in high altitudes. The rule of thumb is that the higher the altitude the coffee is grown in, the less caffeine it develops. The Arabica coffees test at less than 1 percent caffeine. If tea doesn't make you buzz as much as coffee, it's probably because you don't use as much per cup. The standard is 200 cups of tea per pound and 75 to 100 cups of coffee per pound.

G.I. SURPLUS
Q: I don't wish to be an ingrate, but with the government nutrition guidelines pushing whole grains and more-natural foods, why is it that the government regularly gives poor folks

processed cheese and white flour and white rice at food handouts? Seems like those products take more steps to get from farmer to us.

— *Wheatena*

A: The free-food distribution by the U.S. Department of Agriculture is not aimed at improving the nutrition of America's poor. The program serves as a popular method for getting rid of some of the millions of tons of surplus food bought by the government in the price-support programs. This food is stored indefinitely. As warehouse space runs out, the government can either build or buy more space, destroy the food or give it away.

Dumping and burning were tried in the past, but, reasonably enough, this caused public displeasure. Although free distribution costs the USDA money for freight, it is considered good public relations.

The kinds of food that are handed out reflect the USDA's idea of what consumers want. For example, there are millions of pounds of powdered milk stored in 50-pound sacks. It is, says Dan Van Otten of the USDA's Salem office, not the instantly dissolving kind. It takes more effort to mix. This milk is not given out because the USDA received complaints and adverse publicity about handing out "inferior" products. "Americans," says Van Otten, "are evidently used to food with reduced nutritional value." This is why the white flour and rice are handed out. That is what the recipients are used to.

Originally, Cheddar cheese was available in addition to the processed cheese. The Cheddar, explains Van Otten, had been stored so long that some of it had developed mold on the surface. Despite explanations that the mold was not harmful and could be trimmed off, consumers were offended at being given inferior goods. The processed cheese, probably because of a higher salt and preservative content, does not mold as readily.

GREEN CHEESE

Q: I like a bit of aged cheese with my wine. Why, in the face of the label that claims one or two or more years of aging, does my cheese begin to turn green after only two or three weeks in the fridge?

— *Cheese-Green Teeth in Portland*

A: Your fridge is not the optimum storage space for cheese. According to Diane Harlan-Burton, the cheese buyer for Elephant's Delicatessen, refrigerators are not humid enough for the soft cheeses and not dry enough for the hard cheeses.

Once cheese is exposed to the air and to your fingers, it inevitably will develop mold if it survives long enough. Harlan-Burton says no big deal anyway. Just slice the mold off. You could even eat it in most cases and it would not hurt you. Of course, if the cheese gets completely covered with green fuzz, the taste of the mold will begin to permeate the cheese and you probably will prefer to toss it out.

Most cheese actually is made by a process of molding. Blue cheese, for example, is made with penicillin mold. The manufacturers allow rye bread to mold, then dry it, grind it up and inject it into the cheese.

Cheese making is one of those wildly multifarious art forms in which tiny variations in environment or ingredients make astounding differences. True Roquefort can be made only by aging in the high, cool caves of the tiny Roquefort Valley in France. The Oregon Caves are used for aging an altogether different cheese.

Many cheeses are aged in large blocks or wheels and covered with wax or plastic only after they've been cut for sale, whereas many rinded cheeses, says Harlan-Burton, actually develop mold cultures on their surfaces as they age. The rind is washed repeatedly with water, wine or beer, depending on the variety of cheese.

M&M MYSTERY

Q: As a small pebble does lodge in one's shoe and cause much annoyance, so does this question lodge in my brain and cause perplexion:

How is it that m&m's are coated so perfectly? One imagines they must somehow be levitated while being candy-coated. And how do they manage to paint two little m's on each one? And what do the m's stand for, anyway?

— Perplexed

A: "Perplexed" is not alone. Several readers have asked about the various mysteries of the m&m. Now, thanks to the generous help of Hans Fiuczynski, external-relations director for m&m/Mars, Inc., in Hackettstown, N.J., we have a glimmer into these arcane processes.

The chocolate centers, whether plain or peanut, are formed by giant rollers indented with candy shapes. The cooled centers are tumbled—like tumbling agates or other gemstones—to smooth them.

The centers then go through what's called "the panning process." Thousands of little chocolate gobbets at a time are dumped into a huge pan that rotates on an angle, similar to a cement mixer. Corn syrup is added and the gobbets roll around in syrup, coating themselves. Several stages of syrup wallowing, drying and further wallowing build up layer after layer of thin coatings. After a trip through a smoothing pan, where the coated candies tumble and rub together in a polishing process, a final layer of syrup with food coloring is added.

Only one m appears on each candy because there isn't room for two. The m's are not applied with a typewriter but with printing rolls akin to the offset-press system. The unprinted pieces are lined up mechanically and shuffled through a carefully cushioned system (Mars is keen on keeping the candy coating uncracked) with a 99 percent or better printing rate.

The colors are mixed on a prescribed ratio (count out the browns, yellows, etc., from your next pack) and whipped into high-speed packagers.

Mr. Mars started hand-dipping chocolates back in 1911 in the Midwest but really took off when he invented the Milky Way in Minneapolis in the 1920s. The m&m branch of Mars, Inc., kicked off in 1939. The m's stand for Mars and his associate, Murrie, the inventors of the one that melts in your mouth, not in your hand. Mars, Inc., and m&m/Mars are still privately held companies owned by the Mars family.

VIOLENT DIETS?

Q: Recently an in-house publication for a slaughterhouse in Kansas City claimed the majority of wife beaters and child abusers were vegetarians.

Last week when I was grocery shopping at Nature's, I noticed a number of women and children who looked terribly bruised. What's the story, Slice?

— *Almblad*

A: Sounds like hog wallop of the carnivorous variety. There aren't enough vegetarians in the whole country to account for even a third of the gratuitous whomping that goes down. A spokesman for the Men's Resource Center in Portland got a laugh out of the question but says it's ridiculous. Every month, the center treats 50 to 60 men who are batterers, and the spokesperson is convinced that most of them are not vegetarians. Batterers, whether physical, emotional, psychological or sexual, come from all financial and educational classes and all ethnic and racial backgrounds.

The Slicer bets that their diets range from four grains of bulgur daily to still-twitching steaks.

ILLICIT RELATIONS?

Q: A friend of mine who ought to know says that chocolate and cocaine come from the same plant and that when the cocaine trade is finally obliterated (or replaced by something worse) chocolate will disappear from our lives. Say it isn't so, Slice.

— *Choco-freak*

A: It isn't so, and what's this pal trying to do, start a riot? Chocolate comes from the seeds of the *Theobroma cacao* tree, the first term being apt Greek for "food of the gods." Cocaine comes from the leaves of the coca shrub, *Erythroxylon coca*.

10 The Toilet: Our Porcelain Goddess

SPACE VOID

Q: Ever since men and women have been venturing into space, the gnawing and somewhat irreverent question keeps coming to mind: Exactly how do spacecraft toilets really work? How is the obvious disadvantage of the lack of gravity overcome? Are they different for men and women? Is the waste kept in a holding tank, or is it jettisoned in space, creating everlasting orbiting cosmic pollution? What about that ice ball that formed on the last shuttle? Was that dishwater or something yuckier? And exactly what goes wrong with this device that has caused trouble on several flights? What do the Russians do about this problem when they send men into space for months at a time? Could it be that (perish the thought) they are ahead of us in space toilet technology?...Please spare us the generalities with which NASA usually handles this subject.

— *Ehrick W.*

A: The Kremlin has ignored our letters and The Slicer has no information on the Russian approach to voiding in space. The National Aeronautics and Space Administration at Lyndon B. Johnson Space Center in Houston, Texas, provides the following information in a deathless opus entitled *Waste Collection System Workbook WCS 2102C*, from the NASA advanced-training series. The WCS, as a space toilet is known, works the same for males as for females. The unit resembles a Disney World version of the electric chair and is powered by a couple of heavy-duty circuit breakers in the shuttle's electrical system. Besides dealing with what the workbook calls "biowastes," the WCS acts as a disposal for water condensation in the flight deck and airlock and for wash water from the Personal Hygiene Station (the shower). All fluids are collected and stored in a waste-water tank. The only stuff that gets thrown overboard is the gas that accumulates in the trash container; it is blown out through a vent.

The privy portion of the WCS consists of a urinal—basically a funnel attached to a hose—and a commode. The system defies the lack of gravity by the use of air flowing from a pair of fans, which in turn control the directional movement of both liquids and solids on much the same principle as the common household vacuum cleaner. The commode is used in much the same fashion as an "earth facility." The crew member rests on something resembling the seat of a 1942 John Deer tractor and is kept from floating away by foot stirrups, Velcro straps over the legs and a pair of padded bar restraints that lock over the thighs. The commode tank is normally kept sealed by a sliding valve under the seat's 4-inch opening. The crew member adjusts a few levers and dials, causing the vacuum chamber to be pressurized and the sliding valve to open.

Feces enter the chamber drawn by air flowing through holes under the seat. The fecal material is deposited in a specially developed bag liner. The bag is composed of a miraculous material that allows air to pass through but prevents liquid and bacteria from getting out. When the seat opening is again covered by the sliding valve, all the air and moisture are pumped out through yet another sliding valve, leading to an odor-and-bacteria filter that leaves totally dried material in the vacuum of the commode chamber.

The most common breakdown in the system is a wiring failure that glitches the fans. Since the whole system depends on airflow, no fans, no WCS. The emergency substitute—which can also be used if the chamber is simply too full—is a series of sophisticated Ziploc plastic bags. An endless supply of individually wrapped wet wipes is used for washing up afterwards. The designer of the system is listed as one L.W. Lew.

GREEN FALLOUT

Q: How come my pee smells funny shortly after I eat asparagus? It doesn't smell funny the rest of the time.

— Asparagus Lover

A: Rumors of this phenomenon have been floating among The Slicer's acquaintances for years, but "Asparagus Lover" is the first to fess up to a personal involvement. Urologist Robert Barham says the odor is caused by an acid present in the vegetable, and it doesn't happen to everybody. Whether you produce the odor or not is determined genetically.

Anne Hovland of the National College of Naturopathic Medicine in Portland unearthed in the British medical journal *Xenobiotica* an article titled "The Chemical Nature of the Urinary Odor Produced by Man After Asparagus Ingestion," written by Waring, Mitchell and Fenwick of the University of Birmingham in England. The three author-researchers isolated six sulfur alkyl compounds that combine to produce the odor. In testing 800 volunteers, they found that 43 percent had the characteristic ability to excrete these asparagine chemicals in the urine. This inherited ability is a dominant trait. If one of your parents had it, so will you.

GREEN-PEE UPDATE

Q: One more exposition on asparagus and its effect on urinary odor. In England the slang for asparagus is "chambermaid's horror." At first I thought it was due to its phallic shape, but now I realize it was because chambermaids had to empty the gentry's chamber pots. This was all before Sir Thomas Crapper invented the indoor flushing toilet.

— Lance F.

CRAPPED OUT

Q: An update on the "Green-Pee Update " ["The Slice," July 17]: We defy you to find any reference to Sir Thomas Crapper as the inventor of the indoor flush toilet or as the inventor of anything else. Fighting this curious rumor has been a family crusade for years.

Although water closets were used in Britain as early as 1617, no patents were taken out until 1775, by a watchmaker named Alexander Cummings of Bond Street, London. All the elements of the modern flush toilet are incorporated in his invention.

There is no "Crapper," Thomas or otherwise, listed in the *Britannica, Oxford English Dictionary, Columbia Encyclopedia* or *Webster's*—no "crap" either, except as in games.

Alexander Cummings was found in Lawrence Wright's *Clean & Decent, The Unruffled History of the Bathroom and W.C.*, published in 1960 by Viking Press.

— Mary and Herb Park

MORE CRAP

Q: "Crapped Out" ["The Slice," July 14] defied your readers to find a reference to Sir Thomas Crapper as the inventor of the indoor flush toilet. Dr. Laurence J. Peter, author of several books including *The Peter Principle*, includes Thomas Crapper in his 1979 book *Peter's People* as being the uncredited inventor of the modern flush toilet. By 1861, the year Crapper started up his plumbing business in Chelsea, Londoners had been using the water closet for many years, but the W.C. [water closet] wasted so much water that the London board of trade feared the reservoirs would all dry up. After assembling "Crapper's Valveless Water Waste Preventers," which dispensed enough water to flush the toilet, refilled the tank, then shut off automatically, Crapper went on to devise the modern venting system that prevented sewer odors from backing up into the rooms of the building. Wallace Reyburn devoted an entire book to this royal plumber to Kings Edward VII and George V in *Flushed With Pride: The Story of Thomas Crapper*, Prentice-Hall, 1971.

— *Enough of This Crap*

A: A barrage of replies came in from readers answering the challenge of Mary and Herb Park on the subject of Thomas Crapper and the origins of the flush toilet. Several tuned-in types referred to *Flushed With Pride*, and orthodontist R.N.C. was inspired to drop off a copy of the charming pink book at the W.W. office. This small volume is delightfully written and richly illustrated with woodcuts, lithographs and photos, and The Slicer recommends it for bathroom reading.

The disagreement here turns on the phrase "inventor of the modern flush toilet." Crapper's design is definitely the "modern" version. The flush toilet as such is, however, an ancient idea. The Minoan kings had these conveniences 4,000 years ago. The hygiene revival after the Dark Ages was slower in coming. Sir John Harrington, godson of Queen Elizabeth I, installed one version for lusty Liz in 1596 by way of winning her favor after she'd banished him for spreading Italian porn stories. Charles Panati, in his intriguing book *Extraordinary Origins of Everyday Things*, says Harrington blew his chances by writing "a book about the queen's toilet, titled *The Metamorphosis of Ajax*—Ajax being a pun on the word 'jake,' then slang for chamber pot." The queen banished him again, and his flush toilet went unused and forgotten.

Panati credits Alexander Cumming, the same watchmaker designated by the Parks, with the significant patent of an improved form of flush toilet in 1775.

IF YOU SPRINKLE...

Q: Every two or three months I endure the same dilemma, a dilemma it has just occurred to me as one deserving of mention. (It happened to me once again this evening.)

I work and have worked for the last 10 years with the public. I use public facilities. So, in my crude and unabashed manner I "sit" on the "seat"—only to discover that my predecessor has not. And, in her paranoia, has left *many* droplets that form rivulets that make me wet with her leavings, leaving me to dry myself, and, in my empathy for the next unsuspector, the seat. This involves the use of wads of the provided paper.

In an admittedly limited survey I find I'm not alone. What is the psychology of these women? Am I wrong in judging them as uptight, selfish oafs?

— *Wet and Wild*

A: This is far from the first complaint The Slicer has received on the problem. Compulsive crouchers—no doubt traumatized in infancy by tales of crabs, clap and pregnancies contracted from public toilets—have several options to avoid what for them is inconvenience and disgust: (a) lift the toilet seat as men do, before crouching; (b) line the seat with paper; (c) get a "feminine adapter," as those odd funnel entrances for bed pans are known, and stand up to urinate; and (d) clean the seat afterwards.

Now, my dear fellow paranoids, The Slicer has been talking with Dr. Lawrence Foster, the state epidemiologist for the Oregon Health Division. Dr. F. says, "We are really not concerned about public toilets as sources of communicable diseases." The chances of picking up a disease from a toilet seat are very slim, emphasis on "very," according to Foster, unless the seat is visibly contaminated with fresh blood, feces or semen. In any one of those cases—barring a maroon toilet seat—you'd probably notice.

If there is blood or semen in sufficient quantity on the seat and you happen to have an open sore or cut in exactly the spot corresponding to the blood when you sit down, you could conceivably get hepatitis B. The H-B virus, however, will not penetrate normal intact skin, and Dr. F. says he has no evidence that this coincidence has ever actually happened.

If there are feces on the seat, if you get them on your hands, if you don't wash your hands and if you get some particles of feces on your lunch sandwich, you could get a gastrointestinal infection—or maybe salmonellosis. "Urine doesn't pose much risk of transmitting diseases," says Foster. "It's more aesthetically displeasing." About herpes, Dr. F. says the virus attacks mucous membrane by direct contact. The herpes lesion would have to come into contact with the seat—Dr. F. thinks this anatomically unlikely—and there has never been a documented case of anyone contracting the disease this way.

So what about crabs? Extremely unlikely, says the doc. The crab louse wants to stay on the warm human body, and the last place it would choose to drop off is a cool, slick surface. If a louse fell off accidentally, it would immediately leave the seat in search of the next warm body—not too reassuring for passers-by, eh?

In any of those remote possibilities, says Foster, a paper barrier or spread tissue paper provides complete protection. Let's repeat that, for fun: *COMPLETE PROTECTION.*

SPLIT-SEAT SAGA

Q: Why do all public restrooms seem to have toilets with those split seats—the gap in front? My little daughter refuses to use them at her daycare center, which causes her misery and us (grown-ups) mayhem.

— *Fusspot's Mom*

A: You have to sympathize with the poor tyke. Those things must feel like mighty precarious perches for a small person. All public restrooms are required to use toilets with split seats and elongated bowls. The split seat is supposed to prevent the spread of disease. The non-existent front of the seat doesn't get splashed on, etc. Oregon's building code defines a "public" toilet as one that is used by three or more persons other than those related by blood or marriage. Maybe a support bar or arms similar to those available for the handicapped could be attached to help out the small fry.

11 Other Beasts

THE FLY ON THE CEILING

Q: The great Danish muscatologist (scholar of flies), Victor Borge, became obsessed with the following navigational problem toward the end of his life. Government sensibilities being as capricious as they are, he was never able to secure the funding that would be required for anything like an adequate study. At the time that these investigations were forced to a close, there had emerged two major theories as to how flies manage to take off from ceilings, which for simplicity may be called the "taxiing theory" and the "free-fall theory."

According to the taxiing theory, the fly runs along the ceiling until he or she gains sufficient momentum in the horizontal direction, the wings are extended, the fly goes into something like an upside-down glide and then banks neatly over until its landing gear is appropriately oriented with respect to the floor.

The free-fall theory has certainly attained a more vocal following. According to this scenario, at the judicious moment the fly will *leap* off the ceiling, upside down, fall for some distance and then do something like a half twist until it has righted itself. At this point it revs up and soars aloft. The free-fall theory has been considered something of a misnomer by its proponents, who feel it conceals the considerable athletic prowess of the housefly, which they so rightly admire. This dispute, however, has never been resolved to my knowledge. Now, with the resources at your disposal, I would appreciate knowing which, if either, of these theories has been shown to be correct. Also, is it true that these operations on the part of the fly are accompanied by a series of fierce, karate-type cries, which are too high pitched for us to hear?

— A.C. (*Name withheld to prevent embarrassment
to a respected scientist*)

A: With the excellent research resource of a sunny window as a lure for flies, casual observation is sufficient to discover that flies do not glide. The taxiing theory is blatantly absurd and probably based on the same twisted misapprehension of aerodynamics which concluded not long ago that bees cannot fly. Bees and flies function like helicopters. To stay airborne and in motion, a fly's wings beat as often as 200 times per second. The hummingbird's wings, by way of comparison, beat about 75 times a second.

It is precisely their vertical-lateral, topsy-turvy takeoff capacity that makes flies so tricky to swat. The late great auctioneer and big-game smasher, Col. Howard Golly, swore (frequently and colorfully) that the fly leaps backwards on takeoff so the swatter should aim slightly behind the fly to increase the odds of a direct hit.

The order of *Diptera* (two-winged insects) are popular research subjects for biologists. The common housefly, *Musca domestica*, and the blowfly are the special study of muscatologist Vincent G. Dethier. In his charming treatise, *To Know A Fly* (published by Holden-Day, 1962), Dethier explains that flies are available free—he got fifteen years of study out of the progeny of one fly who laid her eggs on an abandoned liverwurst sandwich on his desk one afternoon—as well as cheap to feed. The corpses are easy to dispose of, continues Dethier, and the American Society for the Prevention of Cruelty to Animals is unlikely to concern itself with whether or not the beast was anaesthetized while its wings were being nipped off.

Dethier, a fly fan of the first water, views the ceiling question from a different angle. He writes, "The fly has...wondrous accomplishments...not the least of which is being able to land on the ceiling. For years, controversy has raged as to whether he managed this by executing a half-roll or an inside loop. As a matter of fact he does neither. He flies close to the ceiling in a normal position, then reaches up and back with his front feet till they touch the ceiling, whereupon he somersaults over into position. The incredible nimbleness of the fly is no secret...."

Unfortunately Dethier doesn't describe the mechanics of takeoff. The Slicer, however, sees two possibilities. The free-fall theory may well be correct. Perhaps, though, the cunningly designed critter simply reverses its upside-down landing procedure by hanging on with the front feet, letting the rest of the body swing downward, then letting go and flipping into normal anti-grav position.

FLY ROPING

Q: What the heck is fly roping? I've heard it mentioned a few times ·but always at the tail end of other people's conversations....

— *Frustrated Eavesdropper*

A: There is a whole genre of popular pastimes known as "bar tricks," so called because they usually are performed when the trickster is too drunk to be held responsible for taste, maturity, and so forth. Many of these tricks involve flies. Fly roping is one of the more abstruse. There are a couple of different approaches to the finale but the buildup usually runs along these lines: Snatch a fly out of the air. Hold it in your closed fist without squashing it. Blow on your thumb knuckle (don't ask; I don't know why). Shake the fly in your fist very vigorously to make it dizzy. Throw the fly onto the bar as hard as you can. It should be dazed or even unconscious. While the fly is immobile, make a small slipknot in one end of a thread or a long human hair. Some ropers put the noose over one of the rear legs and tighten it. Other ropers slip it over the fly's head. The danger with this technique is that the fly's head will pop off when the noose is tightened. Hold on to the loose end of the thread and wait for the fly to revive. Watch it fly around on its leash.

THE FLY—DEEP SIXED

Q: About flies. I saw five well-dressed intelligent (looking) men watching a fly crawl feebly out of a mound of white dust on one of the tables at the Virginia Cafe. I was with a squeamish, insect-hating friend and couldn't investigate. They were getting the fly high on cocaine? Or what?

— *Itching with Curiosity*

A: Bar trick with fly. Capture a fly, uninjured (all fly tricks start the same way). Hold the brute by its wings and submerge it in water. Or beer or a kamikaze. The fly isn't fussy. Get someone to bet you that you can't hold the fly under for one minute or five minutes or however long you care to sit there with your pinkies in a glass and then revive it. Put money on it. Put lots of money on it. When the specified time has elapsed, lay the sodden fly on the bar or table. Pour a mound of salt completely covering and surrounding the fly. Wait twenty minutes or an hour, or…Eventually the fly will crawl out of the salt.

Nobody is quite sure why this works. The great muscatologist (student of flies) V.G. Dethier discusses the problem of water loss in the fly in his enchanting book, *To Know a Fly.*

Dethier says, "Flies do not perspire, yet they lose water so readily that they are living virtually in a desert all their lives.... A small creature has much more surface area per unit of body weight than a large creature, and excessive surface area usually means excessive water evaporation...." Dethier's research proves that, unlike that of humans, mongooses and other complex beasts, the fly's thirst is not affected by osmotic pressure or salt concentration but very simply by fluid pressure.

"We have injected into thirsty flies blood, water, concentrated salt, mineral oil and even lighter fluid," writes Dethier. Each of these satisfies the fly's thirst; that is, he no longer drinks water. The lighter fluid kills him, but at least he does not die thirsty." The one exception is the tsetse fly, which lives exclusively on blood and dies immediately if it ingests water.

Dethier also proves that behavior which would get a 12-year-old hauled off to a shrink may earn him sizable research grants as an adult. The great muscatologist explains, by inference, the salt on the bar. It draws off enough excess water so the fly reaches its correct fluid pressure. This evidently enables the beast to resume normal life.

Of course flies breathe air through various trachea holes just like other insects. Why they don't drown is still a mystery to The Slicer.

NO PLAYING POSSUM

Q: With Forest Park in my back yard I confront an opossum or two near my garbage can or chuckling over my dog's dish on the front porch at least once a week. I have shouted, banged garbage-can lids and shown bright flashlights into their eyes, but I have *never* seen an opossum "play possum." Far from pretending to be dead they either slope off into the brush or, if cornered, hiss and snarl with extremely forbidding fangs to back me (and the dog) away far enough to give them a running start. Is it only Arkansas opossums that "play possum"? Do we have a different breed in this neck of the woods?

—*Fangs A Lot*

A: This and several other myths about this intriguing marsupial are punctured by retired PSU professor Tom Burnam of Lake Oswego in his marvelous debunker, *The Dictionary of Misinformation*. Burnam explains, for example, that though the opossum has a prehensile, or grasping, tail, it is not strong enough to support the beast's entire weight, and opossums don't hang upside down from branches by their tails. They do wrap their tails around a branch they're sitting on to help balance and support them.

Another common myth, according to Burnam, is that "both impregnation and birth take place by way of the female's nose. The male, so the myth goes, achieves sexual union by placing his penis in the female's nose; at birth, the female sneezes her young into her pouch. The sexual organs of opossums are, in truth, rather interestingly constructed; the male has a double-headed penis and the female a forked vagina and two uteri. Whether or not this natural back-up system accounts for the proliferation of opossums wherever they are introduced, the fact is that the penis is designed, obviously, to fit the double vagina, not the nostrils."

As for "playing possum," Burnam assures us that the beasts do it rarely and never on purpose. Fight or flight are the opossum's natural response to being chased or threatened. "Occasionally, an opossum may, it is true, collapse in a kind of catatonic state of immobility. But most scientists believe this is not something an opossum does deliberately; it is, rather, a response like the shock a human accident victim suffers [O]ften enough it simply condemns it to death by a predator."

The Slicer suspects that this occasional individual seizure may be a form of narcolepsy (sudden sleep, seemingly induced by excitation or emotion) which has been documented in some dogs and other animals as well as in humans. The idea may be perpetuated because most of us see opossums only on roads and highways where the poor brutes are actually dead.

INVISIBLE SQUAB

Q: Why haven't I ever seen a baby pigeon in the park blocks?
— A. Hasek

A: They are all snugly ensconced in the eaves of The Slicer's house, where it is convenient for their visiting parents to void themselves gleefully onto the sun deck while The Slicer is trying to maintain her freckle ration.

Andy Bartels, the telephone naturalist for the Portland Audubon Society, insists on a less emotional answer. There are some 600 varieties of pigeon on this planet, and the one we call the city pigeon is more correctly known as the rock dove. Bartels says the young are born completely helpless and are tended in the nest for a full month. They don't get out and about until they are fully feathered (full-fledged). You are probably seeing monthlings without recognizing them. They may be slightly smaller than adults, and they usually have a few wisps of yellowish down on their heads. They also have gray bills with pink tips. Adult rock doves have bills the same color as their bodies, though paler close to the face.

According to Bartels, rock doves have "an enormous laying period, usually from early March to late September; if they have a warm nesting area they can even go year-round." These are real family folk. They mate for life—at least no divorce rate has been published—and often have more than one nest. As soon as one set of eggs hatches, they'll lay another set in the nearby second nest.

Bartels recommends an essay on "The Nesting Habits of Rock Doves," by the always excellent E.B. White. It is available in White's volume of essays titled *Points of My Compass*.

The Slicer would like to remind all gourmets and slingshot experts that rock doves were originally imported to this continent as ornamental comestibles. They are also one of only three wild birds in the nation not protected in any way by conservation laws. The others are the English (or house) sparrow and the pesky starling.

Not that The Slicer minds her flock of pigeons. The guano scrapings augment her income handsomely.

A NARROW FELLOW IN THE GLASS

Q: My uncle brought me a pet glass snake from Atlanta when he visited a few months ago. It came with its own terrarium, but I took the snake out to look at it, and it accidentally got the end of its tail caught in my dad's typewriter and cut off. There wasn't a lot of blood or anything. I mean there was some, but not a lot. But the snake seemed to feel OK pretty soon afterwards. And I'm not taking it out of the terrarium any more. So that's the bad part. The weird part is now there's this nub or bump thing growing on the end where the tail used to be. I'm kind of nervous about showing it to my dad until I know why this is happening. Could my snake have cancer?

— *Worried*

A: We won't ask how the critter got into the typewriter. The odds are good that the pet is just regenerating the lost part of its tail. The new growth won't have the same markings or scale pattern as the rest of the animal, and it may end up misshapen or slanting off at an odd angle, but the process is natural and, as these things go, healthy. This is an unusual talent for a snake, but glass snakes are not really snakes at all. They are legless lizards. They have lizard innards and eyelids and external ear openings. Like many lizards, the glass snake has an expendable tail that replaces itself, however clumsily. These harmless bug eaters are natives of the central and southern United States.

INDEX